THE NATURAL WAY
TO
READING

THE NATURAL WAY TO READING

A How-to Method for Parents
of Slow Learners, Dyslexic,
and Learning Disabled Children

Nancy Stevenson

Foreword by C. Keith Conners, Ph.D.

Illustrated by Robert Coolidge

Little, Brown and Company—Boston—Toronto

SECOND PRINTING

T 06/74

The author gratefully acknowledges permission to reprint the quotation on page 237 from R. M. N. Crosby, M.D., with Robert A. Liston,
The Waysiders. Copyright © 1968 by Delacorte Press, reprinted by
permission of Dell Publishing Company, Inc.

Library of Congress Cataloging in Publication Data

Stevenson, Nancy, 1916-
    The natural way to reading; a how-to method for
parents of slow learners, dyslexic, and learning
disabled children.

    1. Reading. 2. Slow learning children. 3. Men-
tally handicapped children--Education--Reading.
I. Title.
LB1050.S75   371.9'044   74-6183
ISBN 0-316-81422-9

Published simultaneously in Canada
by Little, Brown & Company (Canada) Limited

PRINTED IN THE UNITED STATES OF AMERICA

To a twenty-first-century educator,
Stephen K. Hamilton
— who as a cherished friend, inspired,
taught, prodded, and challenged me into
teaching that which I felt to be valid.

FOREWORD

It has been said that language is the feature which sets man apart from all other creatures, and that written language distinguishes civilized man from his more primitive fellows. The process of putting language into symbols, and from symbols back to spoken concepts, is surely one of man's most complex and least understood achievements. Somehow, mysteriously, children learn their native language, learn to associate that language with its written forms, and eventually "decode" the messages so cunningly hidden there by adults.

Much has been written of this process and much accomplished by devout students of the subject; but despite admirable progress, it is disquieting to find that a large percentage of children still fail to learn to read fluently and with pleasure. This book provides a new and unique tool for teaching reading to even the most backward and illiterate. But more than this, the book provides valuable insights into the basic processes involved in reading.

The Integral Phonics Reading Program (IPRP) is a new idea in the field of reading instruction, but it is an idea that draws upon what is known about the basic learning process and the neurologic substrate of that process. In this method, several fundamental principles of learning are utilized in a nontechnical, lucid and interesting manner. The teacher learns along with the pupil how to make the first, basic discriminations needed to begin reading. The task is kept simple, and basic elements are overlearned without boredom until more complex units can be mastered.

In addition to simplifying and overlearning, the child learns the basics of *synthesizing* the primary building blocks (long vowels) with consonants. To aid in this frightening and complicated first maneuver, the child draws upon what he already knows by utilizing auditory associations to the alphabet he has previously acquired. By "auditorizing" the long vowels, previously learned auditory associations acquired from listening to spoken language provide a transition for blending with the less familiar sounds.

A number of valuable memory aids or mnemonic devices are used by the teacher, even with the most primitive steps in the sequence, such as learning to write an "a" so that it is easily distinguished from "o." As one proceeds through the structured lessons one begins to appreciate how carefully the author has taken nothing for granted, has insisted that each and every step in the reading process be fully grasped by the student before he moves on to more complex and unruly coding problems.

The reader will also find a wealth of sound advice regarding the conditions of reward, rapport, and communication necessary for successful teaching. The motivational conditions of the reading relationship between pupil and teacher are fully grasped and incorporated as part of the lessons. This is not, therefore, an ivory-tower method devised by an academician familiar with computer networks and unfamiliar with the living child. The author has *been* there with the child and has sifted her observations into a form that anyone can understand. Perhaps because she is not an academic psychologist but has derived her method from successful teaching with living and learning children, the author is able to impart the basic principles of learning without stuffiness or pedantry.

Processes such as focusing of attention, behavior modification, and multisensory teaching are all employed in this method, and instead of being introduced as separate chapter headings, these topics are skillfully interwoven into the daily lesson plans without burdening the teacher or the child. Because the concepts and methods are presented in the context of actual lessons, the teacher is not distracted by a host of technical terms or definitions. A parent, friend, tutor or teacher can therefore utilize the program without extensive prior background in education or psychology.

C. Keith Conners, Ph.D.
Director of the Beacon School, Brookline, Massachusetts
Director of Child and Adolescent Services,
Human Resource Institute, Brookline, Massachusetts

ACKNOWLEDGMENTS

I wish there were a special way to thank the many individuals who have given me the courage to pull my work together for publication. I can, at least, express my appreciation to the many parents and students whose enthusiasm for my work gave me the incentive to produce this book.

Especially do I thank

— my husband, who patiently tolerated the inconveniences of my endless projects

— my friend of strength, Barbara Pesavento, who helped me weed my thinking

— Bill Redmon, an extremely perceptive neuropsychiatrist involved in the field of reading disorders, who read each part of this book as it developed and helped me open many doors so that I could fit various facets of my work into a broad perspective

— my lawyer friend, Bill Truslow, of Hill and Barlow, who with a light touch nudged me from disorganization to precision

— Helen McElwee, a gifted educator, who suggested I test my materials within her creative program for students with special needs, thus giving me the chance to tighten procedures

— my new friends at Little, Brown: Dick McDonough, who had the vision to realize the need for this book, Lee Workum, Peter Carr and Barbara Pitnof, who had the tedious job of unifying the structural details of *The Natural Way to Reading*

— Nina Wilkins, who with tender care typed the first manuscript that Little, Brown editors could evaluate

— and Blanche Radnor, who with sensitivity kept me out of the pressure cooker by typing those endless pages for final production, thus allowing me the freedom to enjoy putting the pieces together.

CONTENTS

INTRODUCTION

Two-thirds of the school population has had varying degrees of difficulty in trying to acquire reading skills. One-half this number, or one-third of the total, can be guided over an extensive period of time to reading success by well-trained teachers. Of the remaining students, some may be diagnosed as being dyslexic or possessing specific learning disabilities; others may be categorized as lacking maturity or as being simply slow learners. In any case, those burdened with these labels are often the unwitting victims of the battle that rages over reading instruction.

Put another way, of the slightly under sixty million children presently enrolled in public and private schools in the United States, approximately one-third, or just under twenty million, are being left by the wayside as educators have not found adequate methods that can be used for them in the classroom with any predictable success. These students become crippled readers who cannot cope with their textbooks.

This book was inspired by the belief that everyone without major handicaps can be taught to read adequately. I cannot accept the assumption that this large group of children, these twenty million, have to be discards. There are methods in use that do tap the nonreader; however, the problem with these scholarly systems is that they require large numbers of highly skilled technicians, of which there are far too few, to reach the large numbers of disabled readers who need help.

The program I will discuss in detail in this book has been specifically designed to deal with the problem of that discouraged twenty million who might otherwise be left aside. The procedures have been designed so that any adult, parent, or teacher without extra intensive training can help this group of problem readers. The program can be used for the beginning reader or for the severely disabled reader. It does not pretend to be a panacea for *all* reading problems, but it is a system that has worked. It has worked for dyslexic children, for illiterate adults, and for people acquiring English as a second language.

The system, which I call the Integral Phonics Reading Program (IPRP), has been specifically designed so that the beginning reader is not overloaded with directives, which all too often defeat him. Each lesson has special directions that teach the instructor while he teaches the student. The teacher and student commit themselves to thirty minutes a day in a five-day week for one school year.

The IPRP respects the premise that learning to read is a neurological process, a process awesomely complex. It is one more developmental step in the continuum that starts at birth and proceeds throughout the years. At an early stage, the child struggles to turn himself over, in time he sits up, eventually he walks. Each of these involved neurological steps takes place spontaneously with little help from another individual. These steps, while occurring at different times for different children, are "natural" functions. Reading, however, is not a "natural" function, but an intricate, structured activity imposed on the child, and there is no guarantee that successful neurological development of the complex coordination involving auditory and visual responses will take place in a specific child at a specific time.

The IPRP is based on the belief that there is a way to teach reading within the neurological limitations of the child's developmental age. The material was designed to teach reading skills that complement rather than inadvertently negate the neurological development of the student.

I hope that this natural way to reading skills will benefit those twenty million children and alleviate the anguish of their parents while the very necessary but all too often needlessly painful learning process takes place.

For further discussion concerning the neurological basis for this program turn to the appendix.

How the System Works

Long vowels are used exclusively through one-third of the daily lesson section of this book. This method gives the student extensive experience in one type of procedure while building a vocabulary of five hundred words. (Several basic reading systems take the entire school year to build a random five-hundred-word reading vocabulary.) In the IPRP the linguistic patterns of the long vowels are used because the pupil has been exposed to these letter sounds throughout his preschool years. When the child sees the letter *a*, he learns that its sound is going to be the same as it is in the alphabet. These long vowels say their names. If the Integral Phonics Reading Program had started with short vowels, the child would consciously have to remember that the letter *a* does not sound like the letter *a* in the alphabet. He has to remember it has the sound of the *a* as in *tack* and that short *e* has the sound of the *e* as in *pet*. Sounds of short *i*, *o*, and *u* have to be anchored also.

The child has a difficult enough time remembering the sounds of the twenty-one other letters (consonants) of the alphabet that do not say their names. For example, the letter *w* sounds more like the alphabet name of *y*. Is it any wonder that many students hearing the word *wait* think this word starts with *y*?

Every consonant in the English alphabet has one or more sounds. The child has to bring to mind instantaneously what the sound is going to be as he meets each consonant. By relieving the child of changing the familiar names of the vowel sounds to other sounds, one major part in the analyzing process has been simplified. Later, when the first steps of reading have become automatic, the student is ready to master the short vowels.

Other programs that introduce the long vowels in the first steps of reading spend a very short time in this area. They also use multisyllable words as well as suffixes in the introductory stages of reading. The added visual burden of these structures is one more complexity that can temporarily be eliminated for the beginning reader. These complexities are not introduced in the Integral Phonics Reading Program until the student has mastered the prerequisite skill, that of blending the correct consonant and vowel sounds into whole-word form.

This blending process is a simple task for some children but is extremely difficult for those whose nervous systems have not reached optimal development. The neurological task of combining a consonant (any of the other twenty-one alphabet letters) with a long vowel is as difficult for the beginning reader as is the first step the child takes when he begins to walk. Each time the child combines a consonant with just the long *a* he is accomplishing a task as arduous as taking a first walking step. Making the sounds of *ba, ca, da, fa,* etc., is a complicated neurological achievement. Then the child is expected to combine the twenty-one consonants with the long vowel *e,* plus *i, o,* and *u.* Here is the same torture all over again.

It is incomprehensible to those who did not have to struggle through these developmental reading steps that enunciating the consonant-vowel combination should be difficult, just as it is incomprehensible to those who can play the piano without reading music notes that this musical facility should be impossible for others.

You may think there are very few children who are handicapped to the point where they cannot readily blend a consonant to a vowel. In my experience I find that large numbers of beginning readers have blending difficulties. Instead of this stumbling being a deviation from the norm, I propose that it is a normal neurological developmental step. The beginning walker stumbles; so does the beginning reading blender stumble. One holds the hands of an awkward toddler when he learns to walk. The stumbling blender must be guided into repeating the vowel aloud, then holding the sound in his mind while he sounds the consonant and blends it to the vowel.

In the IPRP the child is taught to look at the word, focus his eyes on the first vowel rather than the first consonant, and then name it aloud to the teacher. When the student focuses on the word *rake,* he repeats aloud the letter *a.* Then the teacher points her pencil to the letter *r.* The student sounds the *r* and blends it with the long *a.* If the child starts with the consonant sound, which is the procedure in other programs, he has difficulty blending it with the vowel sound because he has not made that *recent* conscious effort to repeat the vowel sound. The vowel sound is not fresh in his experience even if he is looking at it. Not until he has consciously said the vowel out loud can he successfully combine the consonant with it.

It seems reasonable not to introduce words that vary in vowel sound until the student begins to understand how to handle basic patterns. As the child progresses, the parent and the teacher gain an appreciation of the complicated coordinating mechanisms that make a successful reader. These adults become sympathetic instead of impatient with the child who must be allowed time and be given the right tools so that he may build his skills according to his own learning pattern.

1

Questions and Answers

ONE: FOR PARENTS WHO ARE CONCERNED WITH THEIR CHILD'S READING SKILLS

Many parents hesitate to ask their child's teacher frank questions which they feel might be embarrassing; or they may be at a loss to know what to ask that would help them better understand school problems. I have tried to anticipate these questions and to give the answers in the following material. The second section of questions and answers is compiled for the individual who will be teaching the Integral Phonics Reading Program.

What Is Meant by the Term "Learning Disabled?"

The term "learning disabled" is a label given to a type of student who seems to be intelligent but is unable to learn academic material readily. A precise definition of the label at this time is not possible because specialists in the fields of education, medicine, and psychology are not in full agreement as to the classification of this learning problem syndrome.

The term "learning disability" is often used interchangeably with the terms "dyslexia," "perceptual handicap," "maturational lag," "minimal cerebral dysfunction," and a few other confusing titles. Whatever terminology is used, the layman is still caught in confusion. The important point to keep in mind is that many people are finally looking at a phenomenon that has existed throughout the centuries. No longer are we trying to sweep the problem out of sight. We are at last realizing that there are people with adequate intelligence (sometimes measurably very high intelligence) who have an exceedingly difficult time in learning to read, write, and spell. These people have no overt deficiency in eyesight and no obvious problem in brain function. They just cannot master with ease the complicated task of reading and the broader aspects within the language arts area. In the past, these people may have been labeled slow, stubborn, lazy, or rebellious, thus compounding the problem by creating emotional instability in the victims. Many through mismanagement have become nonproductive adults.

If you ask what numbers of people fall into this nebulous category of learning disabilities, you will find that some educators and scholars have given various estimates ranging from ten to as high as seventy-five percent of the population.[1] Some specialists consider that all functionally illiterate people have some form of dyslexia. With careful training, these people overcome their problems and become successful adults, many graduating from college with honors.

There seems to be agreement among specialists that the person who is labeled dyslexic has trouble associating the correct letter sounds with the letters he sees. The problem involves processing in both the auditory and visual fields.[2] These people may receive auditory and visual stimuli but their ability to transmit the original information accurately is faulty.

The difficulty appears to be a breakdown in the process of associating a visual symbol with some piece of previously learned knowledge, so that when recall is required, the symbol is reproduced in garbled form. The dyslexic student has directional decision problems. Such letters as *b* and *d*, as well as *p* and *q*, may be reversed, along with the reversing of words like *on* and *no*.

Later, when trying to spell, these students have trouble remembering the order of letters in words.[3]

While learning to read, all children experience some difficulty in letter and word reversal. With continued practice the child soon overcomes his difficulty. Only if the condition continues to the point where the child does not make progress in reading skill is there need for concern.

Dyslexics may have difficulty in holding the auditory or visual stimuli long enough to permit accurate transmission of the information.[4] Or the transmission facility itself may not have the strength needed to allow for precise output of stored information.[5] The question to examine is whether this predicament is a normal characteristic of a specific number of people, just as having brown eyes as opposed to blue eyes is characteristic of a specific number of individuals, or whether the phenomenon being described is a malfunction.

Could we have been expecting all brains to respond to certain types of teaching instead of finding alternative teaching methods to unlock the electrochemical response of many kinds of brains? In the future we may give the disabled learner a new label that does not suggest a type of faulty activity. We have, at least, progressed to the point where we are admitting that not all people can learn by methods that are inflicted upon them.

Why Has the Term "Dyslexic" Been Used Throughout This Book?

There is so much heat in the debate as to what term should be used to describe the disabled reader that I find it difficult to use any term comfortably.

[1] R. M. N. Crosby, M.D., with Robert A. Liston, *The Waysiders* (New York: Delacorte Press, 1968), p. 18.

[2] Ralph D. Rabinowitch, M.D., "Reading Problems in Children: Definition and Classifications," in Kenney and Kenney, eds., *Dyslexia* (Saint Louis: C. V. Mosby, 1968), p. 8.

[3] MacDonald Critchley, *The Dyslexic Child* (London: William Heinemann Medical Book, 1970), p. 44.

[4] Ibid., p. 88.

[5] Samuel Torrey Orton, M.D., *Reading, Writing and Speech Problems in Children* (New York: W. W. Norton, 1937), p. 145.

I have borrowed the label "dyslexic" because of my admiration for those neurologists who have realized that there have been a large number of intelligent people who should not have been forced to meet defeat because of being pressed into ill-fitting molds. Most of these courageous neurologists have used the expression "dyslexia."

Do the Majority of Educators Agree with Each Other?

In every professional field, you will find adamant divergence of opinion based on a variety of philosophical differences. In the field of education, a distinguished scholar may advocate methods of teaching that are diametrically opposite to those supported by another scholar.

As a layman, of course, you become confused. Who should you believe? If your child is having a successful learning experience, you can assume that the school has found a good way to teach him or her. If your child is not succeeding, either his teachers have not as yet found a way to tap his ability or they feel he lacks ability to adapt to their methods of teaching.

If you question the suitability of methods used for the floundering child, you may experience an unpleasant confrontation. There are a few teachers who are secure enough to admit that the wrong program has been used to teach your child. Often teachers take any interrogation to mean they are inadequate as teachers and respond to the parent with anger. No one ever is comfortable with the thought that he or she may be doing an inadequate job.

If a Teacher Teaches Reading, Should Parents Assume He or She Is an Authority?

Many parents assume that if a teacher is certified, he or she is an authority in reading. They surmise that a teacher has spent four years in college pursuing the fine details of teaching reading. Check the college curricula to see how much time the student spends on reading courses. An M.D. degree does not make a heart specialist. A bachelor's degree does not make a reading specialist, a mathematics, a language arts, a social studies, or a science specialist. These are all required subject areas the teacher must teach in the elementary grades. Then, to compound the problems, the teacher finds that no matter how many teaching-methods courses have been digested, he or she still has to have a great deal of knowledge in subject matter in order to simplify the material for beginning students. The elementary school textbooks do not do this job for the child or the teacher.

A young person just out of college can be a very adequate teacher, but he or she cannot be expected to be an authority in any subject area, at least until he or she has had wide experience and years of study.

When the person reaches the point where he is designated an authority, you may find him to be knowledgeable in a specific area, but that does not mean you have to subscribe to the school of thought this person represents.

Today, such a vast amount of information is available that one person or one group cannot cover all facets. There can be no finite answers. If you are not satisfied with the recommendation of a so-called authority, you owe it to yourself to investigate other avenues.

What Does the Integral Phonics Reading Program Offer That Other Programs Do Not?

The main features of the Integral Phonics Reading Program are:

1. A daily lesson plan for teacher, parent, or tutor to use for teaching reading.
2. Long vowels used exclusively to build a five-hundred-word reading vocabulary before other phonic integrals are introduced.
3. Difficult concepts, such as multisyllable words and suffixes, not introduced until the student feels competent in the first steps of decoding.
4. No pictures (preventing guesswork).
5. Focusing on the first vowel instead of the first letter when meeting new words. (Involves the use of the Seven Special Steps, integral to the entire program. The Steps are described following Lesson 2.)
6. Emphasis on making a conscious effort rather than relying on automatic recall when mastering the technique of blending.
7. Explanations of student reactions at various stages during lesson periods.

The Integral Phonics Reading Program is designed to simplify the teaching of reading so that any adult who likes children and who is willing to follow written directions can teach a child to read.

Why Is the Procedure That Is Stressed in the Seven Special Steps So Important?

The Integral Phonics Reading Program has been designed to strengthen the brain pathways used for reading and for spelling. When a word is read, the printed symbol has to register on the primary visual area of the brain. The stimulus is transferred to the part in the brain called the *angular gyrus*. This area in turn signals the section of the brain that must arouse the auditory form of the word before it can be processed.[6] The Seven Special Steps were developed to respect and to reinforce this natural process. This procedure is especially important for those people who cannot cope with the entire configuration of the word.

In the Integral Phonics Reading Program, the eye is trained to select a small unit from a word. The brain is not forced to deal with a large grouping of letters that do not register with enough strength to allow for further processing, as is the case in the whole-word (look-and-say) procedure.

The Seven Special Steps cause the individual consciously to use a technique to strengthen the brain pathways involved in reading. In a short time, the procedure becomes automatic. Pointing at words and mouthing the words act as stimuli to arouse the auditory area of the brain, which must react in order to complete reading action. Many teachers have been trained to discourage the mouthing of words in the mistaken belief that this procedure slows reading growth. Instead, these teachers are penalizing the person who does not respond to the look-and-say method of reading.

Those who have worked intensively with the disabled reader will immediately question the validity of sequencing in the Seven Special Steps. The dyslexic student has such confusion

[6] Norman Geschwind, "Language and the Brain," *Scientific American* (April, 1972), p. 79.

establishing correct directional sequencing that teaching the pupil to focus on the vowel first would seem to be complicating matters. This procedure can be logically but very technically explained; more important is the fact that the technique works. Before condemning the reasoning behind the IPRP procedure, try it, then make the decision whether it is workable or not.

Keep in mind one point when you hear the argument favoring the need to start with the first letter in the word in order to establish left-right sequencing. The traditional approach would seem to prevent mistakes like reading *was* for *saw;* however, it does nothing to help the child stop inverting the letters *n* and *w* as well as *n* and *u,* a problem that is related to the reversing you are trying to cure.

Much of what we do to bring the student reading success cannot be backed by pure logic. There is still too much we do not know about how the brain processes information. If the child learns to read without trauma, the procedure used should be considered valid.

Why Are Short Vowels Troublesome for Students?

During the preschool years, the child enunciates the short vowels in many of the words he uses, but he is not conscious of their tones as isolated sounds. This is not the case with long vowels. Unless the child has been a victim of deprivation, he has listened to people talk about the alphabet for several years. A doting grandmother may have taught the alphabet song or the child may have heard the names of the long vowels in records and nursery rhymes.

Educational television and kindergarten experiences have given the student added exposure to the printed shapes of the letter sounds. This exposure takes place intermittently over a period which Piaget calls the "preoperational years" (two to seven).[7] The alphabet *a* says *a* (long *a*) to the child. This is obvious knowledge that he is able to comprehend. However, if the child tries to absorb the information about short vowels in the early years, he is hampered by his inability to cope with what Piaget calls "conservation."[8] Short *a* does not seem to be what it says it is, just as that tall beaker of water seems not to have the same amount of water as was in the fat drinking glass.

Many educators feel that students often cannot manage the phonics of the short vowels until they can handle abstractions; therefore, in the meantime, they proceed to teach words by sight, hoping the child will remember the words as he did those repetitious nursery rhymes.

Instead of discarding phonics because of the troublesome short vowels, I have capitalized on the child's acquired knowledge of long vowels that say their names. These are the sounds that cause letters to become words with meaning. These vowels are the only parts of the word that make sense to the child. The first vowel remains reliably the same alphabet name sound, allowing the child time to wrestle with those confusing consonants.

In the IPRP, the student spends a long period of time with what is for him a logical sequence, thus laying the groundwork that will allow him to face the short vowels with a minimum of trouble. Also, by this time, his maturation level has reached the operational point (seven to eleven years) that Piaget addresses.[9]

[7] Jean Piaget, *The Psychology of Intelligence* (London: Routledge & Kegan Paul, 1971), p. 123.
[8] Ibid., p. 131.
[9] Ibid., p. 123.

The relevance of the theory behind the Integral Phonics Reading Program is basically incidental to the teacher. The important factor is that the program works for many students. The Seven Special Steps grew from necessity not from theory. They help the child through the short- and long-vowel patterns.

If My Child Can Give Me the Sounds of the Short Vowels,
Why Can't He Read the Words with These Vowels?

Many students come to me with the ability to recite all the varieties of sounds of the letters of the alphabet. They can often recite the rules applying to the short and long vowels and they may even know the list of two hundred words used most often in basic reading books. The pupils have had conscientious teachers who have worked hard to drill this information into them. The tragedy comes when these students try to read the printed pages. They misread enough of the words so that comprehension is impossible. They seem to have no way to analyze the new words they meet even though the rules to unlock the words are available.

Unfortunately, this type of student, who cannot respond to current methods, has not been tuned in to a simplified, consistent procedure that will help him decode the mystery of words. The Seven Special Steps, if used repeatedly, give the student tools to use while he puts all his information together.

Why Is So Much Time Spent on the Long Vowels?

The child's fine auditory discrimination ability may not be highly developed when he starts school. If a child has poor motor coordination, the condition is quite obvious. The astute teacher gives special work to the child who needs help while he develops better motor skills. On the other hand, that same teacher may have no idea that the child who manifests no gross hearing problem may have trouble distinguishing among the fine differences in the sounds of short *a, i,* and *e.*

The range in sound change between the long-vowel sounds is much greater than is registered when short vowels are used. The beginning reader has to acquire so many new techniques, that there is no need to burden him with fine auditory discrimination tasks.

There are enough long-vowel words to formulate a good body of reading material for practice before the child has to cope with the mechanics of more precise auditory sorting.

If We Can Make Superstar Readers, Why Can't We at Least Make
Adequate Readers Out of the Rest of the Population?

We have created superior systems to train a certain number of students to become superstar readers. We have also analyzed the mechanical steps needed in athletic games to produce superstar athletes.

Forty years ago, precision athletics was in its embryonic stage. Today, every move the athlete makes is based on previously analyzed and perfected strategy. Even so, these training techniques fit only the person who has a certain type of aptitude. If the methods were applied to a whole population, no one would expect perfect performance.

We can build superstar athletes and we can build superstar readers. However, there is no great crisis if we cannot teach all people to be excellent athletes, whereas an individual's livelihood is in jeopardy if he has not acquired good reading skills.

Educators have not been able to simplify instructional procedures to meet the needs of people who do not respond to current methods. It is just as difficult to develop systems to train these people as it would be to find techniques to make every person become a competent athlete.

Why Did Educators Exchange the Old-Fashioned Phonics for the Sight Method?

Educators have always been embarrassed by the statistics that reveal the appalling numbers who are functionally illiterate. Periodically, a new school of thought flourishes that promises a panacea for reading difficulties.

During the 1920s, most educators of the school systems in the United States were convinced they should change their programs to the look-and-say whole-word method.[10] However, this approach to reading brought no more success to disabled readers than did previous methods. Many teachers, realizing the limitations of the whole-word recognition method, quietly taught some phonics along with their other material.

Then in 1955, Rudolf Flesch's book, *Why Johnny Can't Read*, startled the nation. The bestseller jolted parents into realizing that many of their children were crippled readers. In fact, the horrors of the turn-of-the-century reading failures seemed no worse than those of the 1950s in spite of years of radical changes in the method of teaching reading. Not being exposed to the historical picture of how the look-and-say reading method developed, these parents took at face value Flesch's recommendation that old-fashioned phonics would remedy reading problems.

Parents requested new phonics programs for their children.[11] Publishers began to vie with each other to see who could bring back phonics in the most palatable form.

Many people have assumed that phonics in any form could be the cure-all for the nonreader. It is true that to become a good reader and speller a student has to acquire a knowledge of phonics. Just any program of phonics, however, will not necessarily lead to success. Much material that has been developed is too complicated for the child to absorb and too complicated to teach successfully.

In 1937, Samuel T. Orton, the famous neurologist, along with clinicians who had worked with disabled readers, stated that the student needs to acquire knowledge in phonics to acquire sound reading skills.[12]

These people were very careful to explain that the phonics methods must be skillfully programmed for the developmental needs of the student.

[10] Charles C. Walcutt, ed., *Tomorrow's Illiterates: The State of Reading Instruction Today* (Boston: Little, Brown, 1961), p. 18.

[11] Jeanne S. Chall, Ph.D., *Learning to Read: The Great Debate* (New York: McGraw-Hill, 1967), pp. 290–291.

[12] Orton, op. cit., pp. 158–159.

Educators are still groping to find solutions that will unlock every type of ability. As yet no one system has been developed that will guarantee that all children in the classroom will learn to read.[13]

Can All Students Learn By a Sight Method if They Apply Themselves?

There are many people who cannot learn to read by the look-and-say or sight method.[14] This failure is not caused by lack of intelligence. These people usually are very logical thinkers who will have successful recall only after they have consciously registered information by relating it to other learned material.[15] If these individuals do not record data in their minds by inductive reasoning, they proceed to memorize for today but cannot recall by tomorrow.

If you read *The Waysiders* by R. M. N. Crosby, M.D., and Robert A. Liston, you will begin to realize what a complex neurological feat the process of reading is.

In What Way Are Many Phonics Programs Too Difficult for the Disabled Reader?

An in-depth study of phonics and phonetics can be extremely fascinating but complicated. There are many factors that can change the sound or structure of a word, and when you try to explain these variations to the beginner, mass confusion and discouragement can result. Making the decision of which bare essentials should be presented is usually based on theory rather than on what has been tested on disabled readers.

The selection of integrals of phonics that have been incorporated into the IPRP was made after a long period of trial and error. If several students struggled over the same units, I had to find a more simplified presentation or put the information aside until it fit into a logical slot. Many times this meant that the strict rules of phonics had to be suspended temporarily because the students had not reached the maturational level necessary for coping with the material. For example, the statement that a vowel has the long sound in any one-syllable word containing two vowels seems like an easy rule to teach. When you begin to analyze the various factors involved in this statement, you can appreciate the many brain pathways used to process this information. For the dyslexic with specific weaknesses, that simple statement cannot be implemented because of its hidden complexity.

Many phonics teaching materials seem easy at first glance but are really so complicated that students soon give up the struggle.

One typical example of the unrealistic method of presentation of a phonics unit involves the integral *oo*, which can have sounds as in *pool, book, door,* and *blood*. Some teachers, having seen the lack of success when the student struggles with the comparison of these sounds, decide that phonics and phonetics are too difficult to teach in the early grades.

In the IPRP only one sound is given at a time. The second sound of the integral is not pre-

---

[13] Crosby and Liston, op. cit., p. 32.

[14] Helen R. Lowe, "The Whole-Word and Word-Guessing Fallacy," in Charles C. Walcutt, ed., op. cit., pp. 87–114.

[15] Ian M. L. Hunter, *Memory* (Baltimore: Penguin Books, 1968), p. 293.

sented until the student has used the first information over a considerable length of time. The sound in a specific set of words has been processed enough times so that automation has taken place by the time another sound of the configuration is introduced.

If My Child Turns Out to Be an Able Sight Reader, Why Should He Start with a Phonics Program?

You may have heard that those students who read easily by the look-and-say method do not need to be bogged down by the mechanics of phonics.

These students may not need phonics for reading skills, but it should be pointed out that the child's spelling may suffer if he or she is not exposed to phonics.

A number of studies have revealed that a good many students who have acquired reading success easily, without phonics drill, are very poor spellers.[16] Those few who have escaped spelling disaster have been found to be perceptive enough to see the phonic components of words. They have been able to teach themselves a type of phonics information.

If the sight reader finds he eventually uses phonics anyway, why not expose him at an early age along with those who must have these materials to succeed?

Why Do Some Reading Specialists Tell Us That Phonics Drill Is Not Necessary in the Beginning Grades?

Many teaching specialists will tell you they can teach the child to read without going through the decoding process. These teachers may use phonic or linguistic materials. In the procedures these teachers use, oral phonics drill that involves conscious-level participation from the student is replaced by activity that requires the student to receive the material and then transmit the information on an *automatic* basis rather than requiring that the child work consciously to recall the stored information.

Their method exposes the child to oral work with words like *hat, rat, mat,* followed by words like *can, fan, ran,* etc. The sounds are repeated while the child looks at the words in print. The child repeats the words in oral drill, and with constant repetition the words become registered in his mind. This process is mostly visual and sound bombardment. No specific concentrated *conscious effort* on the part of the child is involved. The whole performance is quite successful for a while. The child may even be able to remember to tell you that these are short *a* words. Then the teacher exposes the children to words like *set, met, let,* and all the other short *e* words. Along comes short *i* in *sit, fit, kit.* By this time a number of children begin to run into trouble. The sight and sound of these short vowels do not pop into their minds so readily now that many words are involved. The big guessing game begins for these youngsters. If there are enough pictures in the book, the students become quite adept in the guessing game. However, when the multisyllable words have to be dealt with, many children become hopelessly confused. These students have no information they can tap that will help them make a decision about how to tackle new words.

[16] Walcutt, op. cit., pp. 12–14.

Isn't Phonics Training Too Complicated for the Beginning Reader?

Phonics, training need not be arduous if the process is simplified. Without having made the *conscious effort* that much of the phonics training requires, many children are hampered in meeting eventual reading success.

When learning about the sight and sound of a new phonic element, the student has to make a *conscious* association with the new unit in relation to a previously learned experience; otherwise the holding power of the reception of the material will be temporary.

You use conscious associative learning daily. If you wanted to make a concerted effort to connect the name of a newly introduced person, you would say, "How do you do, Mr. Longfellow." You could then consciously say to yourself this man has a long, thin face and he is a fellow. I will try to associate his long, thin face with his name when I have to recall who he is.

This conscious association experience may take place so successfully and quickly with some types of students that it seems as if they are not actually going through the process. With other children, this new associative learning experience has to be repeated in a variety of ways in order to have the material make a lasting impression. This very process of making a conscious effort seems like a torturous procedure for some students. Keep in mind that when these students master the technique, they have acquired a skill that they will put to use with every new experience.

Can the Integral Phonics Reading Program Be Used for Any Disabled Reader Regardless of Age?

This book was originally designed specifically for disabled readers aged six through eleven years. These students would range from first-grade repeaters up through the fifth grade. I have used the basic system for individuals through thirty-six years of age.

The whole program is much easier to use if the student can read *less* than fifty words. Often the pupil has been drilled by conscientious teachers so that after four years he does know the two hundred most often used words in basic reading books. The student reads those words by sight so that when he meets them in this book he does not use that important decoding skill, the technique that is going to pull him out of his reading problem.

For the student who has this small sight vocabulary, the teacher will have to check in this book the words on the lists that the student cannot read and use these to teach decoding skill. This type of pupil prospers best by spending most of his time on spelling and dictation rather than reading the stories several times.

When working with the layer-cake words, the teacher would have to use words that are unfamiliar in sound and sight, such as, *cove, dome, lobe, dole, gale, bale,* and *vile.* These are words the student would presumably not be able to read by sight.

The important point is that your disabled reader must learn to analyze or decode his words before he can meet reading success. This starts out being a slow, labored process. In the long run, the procedure is not slow. Better that at the end of one year he can read twenty-five hundred words on a decoding basis than that he take four years to sight-read two to three hundred words. The decoding student does automate his reading into a natural, free-flowing process. The length of time that this development takes depends upon the severity of his original problem and also upon how much intensive work is done with him.

If the Child Is Taught One System in School, Will Home Activity in Another System Confuse Him?

If the child is not succeeding, he cannot be any worse off than he is. Some other program is not going to make more confusion of his present confusion. If you follow the Integral Phonics Reading Program conscientiously, you will find that the child seems to improve his schoolwork even though the Integral Phonics Reading Program is, at first, quite different from the school program. The child's academic achievement at home proves to him he does have ability after all. This seems to give him a confidence that flows back into school.

When you start the Integral Phonics Reading Program, explain to your child that what you are teaching him will, at first, not be the same as his schoolwork. Eventually, he will see how it all fits together.

Is It Better for the Beginning Reader to Use Printing or Cursive Writing?

Some educational specialists feel it is easier for the student to learn cursive script writing rather than printing when he starts to put words on paper. These teachers state that cursive writing allows much more freedom because the child uses gross motor activity instead of the constrained fine-muscle action that printing demands.

Over the years I have tried both techniques. I cannot say whether control of letter formation is made any easier for the poorly coordinated student by large cursive movement or by fine printed form. I feel that printing lends itself to a consistent directional configuration that can be mastered with minimal confusion. Another point I have taken into consideration is that when the child leaves the tutor after tutorial cursive writing instruction, he goes back to the classroom, where his peer group is printing and the teacher's board work is in printed form. Here he meets the confusion of two systems.

The dyslexic students I have tutored have a heavy load to contend with when facing a printed page. Teaching the spelling of those words a dyslexic student has learned to decode is a most difficult feat. I find the student can best associate the letter shapes with sounds if they are similar to the printed page he has been viewing. At a later date, many dyslexics who have succeeded in reading have had to make a temporary adjustment when the teacher begins to use cursive on the board. Because there are students who have trouble learning to read cursive writing, it would seem prudent to avoid two kinds of letter shapes in the early stages of reading instruction. My goal has been to eliminate as many directives as possible until the brain pathways have been strengthened. (You must keep in mind, however, that a gifted teacher works miracles when combining various techniques. If he or she is succeeding with your child, you cannot condemn the method used.)

You will soon see that in the Integral Phonics Reading Program, the shapes of the printed letters lend themselves to anchor phonics concepts. That long, loud round *o*, who is first in line, has a friend beside him that must be quiet. This friend is ɑ, made just like *o* only he leans on a stick.

In later lessons, the student finds that silent *a* has his turn to speak when he becomes the first vowel in line. Now ɑ who leans on his stick has a stick friend right next to him. This is the letter *i*. The two sticks stand beside each other. This stops the confusion of trying to rely on the visual memory decision of which letter comes first, ɑ or *i*. The student uses the shape of his printed letters to establish phonic and linguistic concepts. Every step builds upon previously learned experience instead of demanding a new purely visual stimulation experience.

By the time the student is ready for cursive writing, much groundwork has become automatic. He is now ready to make the new shapes used in cursive writing that flow from the printed form of letters in the system I have developed.

Why Does My Child Read Poorly from Mimeographed Material?

When a person is learning to read, the process of connecting the letter symbol he sees with the correct sound that he must remember from previous instruction is extremely complicated.[17] When many variables are added to the reading task, the person whose nervous system does not work with efficiency meets defeat instantly.

The mimeographed sheet of printed words often is a variable that adds an extra load on the heavily taxed beginner. The letters on that printed sheet may stand out distinctly to you, but look again. If you compare carefully the print in a reading book with the mimeographed material, you will see a slight fuzz bordering each letter. Carbon copies have more blur even though you, as a successful reader, can easily distinguish the words. This seemingly slight distraction becomes a major problem to the disabled reader. Another factor that distracts the student is the variation in the style of the print.

I have found it most important to eliminate mimeographed or carbon copies of material until the student becomes familiar with decoding skill. Even after a student becomes a successful reader, the use of minimally clear work sheets should not be permitted.

Why Do Educators Use Terms That Are Not Familiar to the Layman?

Every profession has its set of terms that seem to be used to confuse the public. The jargon that educators have developed is often not familiar to the lawyer and vice versa. The terms are not, in most cases, created to confound the layman; they are really shorthand words that speed the discussion. I could say, "Pick up the round red object that is on the flat board resting on four sticks." Or I could say, "Pick up the apple from the table." By using single words to describe objects I can make a sentence with seven words instead of sixteen. Many of the terms educators use to simplify discussions among themselves often cause confusion for the general public.

When you become familiar with the mechanics of phonics, you will add new terms to your vocabulary. To ask you to memorize new terminology would be defeating if you are a novice.

---

[17] Edwin M. Cole, M.D., *Specific Reading Disability: a Problem in Integration and Adaptation* (Pomfret, Conn.: The Orton Society Reprint Series, 1951), p. 6.

I shall not use "phoneme," "grapheme," "cognitive ability," "perceptual disability," "basal reader," "cobasal readers," "modality," and many, many other words that would cause you constantly to refer to a glossary.

The only term I shall use quite often that may be unfamiliar to you is "decode," which will explain itself as you progress. Decoding is an analyzing procedure. A secret message may need to be decoded. Words, like secret messages, have to be decoded, also.

Why Doesn't the Teacher Use a Reading System That Will Fit My Child's Learning Pattern?

Parents often assume that there is a true science to the methods of teaching reading. If you read Dr. Jeanne Chall's book, *Learning to Read, the Great Debate,* you will discover the variety of reading programs that are available. Each educational publisher presents a method that often differs quite radically from another's. There is no specific scientific method that fits the abilities of large percentages of children.

School budgets very rarely allow money for several full sets of basic readers to be used for each class. In most schools, the teacher is given one set of books that he or she finds may be productive for at best half the class.

The stories in the student's reading book are based on a specific reading method. If the child cannot learn by the method used in his book, the book becomes useless when another method is tried. The teacher cannot teach another method if the child has no material to read to fit an alternative program. This book problem applies to first- and second-grade reading material. After the child has a clear understanding of how he has built his reading vocabulary of about twenty-five hundred words, he can then usually read from any set of books geared to his grade level.

Why Doesn't the Teacher Explain to the Parents the Dilemma He or She Faces When Teaching Reading?

Many teachers have never faced the reality or have no realization that they have not found a way to make the textbooks assigned to them work the magic they would like.[18] These teachers become defensive, thinking they have failed. The textbook must be right, they reason. After all, it was written by a famous educator. Even those teachers who have finally come to understand that mass-production methods of teaching reading do not work, often are unable to communicate this information to parents.

The few parents who have insight into the problems have great difficulty in communicating their message to the community finance committees, who in turn would have the frustration of selling the idea of a tax increase to those very parents who deplore the state of affairs in the classroom.

[18] Gilbert Schiffman, "Program Administration within a School System," in John Money, ed., *The Disabled Reader* (Baltimore: Johns Hopkins Press, 1966), p. 255.

When the School Orders New Books, Can the Teacher Have a Choice?

This depends on the school system. Even if the teacher has a choice, he or she still usually can have only one program for his or her use. Many teachers are not happy with any of the materials made available to them, and they usually have no one to advise them of the advantages of various alternatives.

It is very time-consuming to keep abreast of the strengths and weaknesses of the new materials on the market.

Do All the Stories for Beginning Readers Have to Be So Dull?

We now have numbers of books for the beginning reader that are appealing to youngsters. Many students, however, are not learning to read these books any better than the dull *Run, Jack, Run* books.

Unfortunately, most of these reading books assume the child can learn to read if he is exposed to words often enough. This is still the look-and-say method that works for some and produces dismal failure for others.[19]

No matter what system is created, an author has a very limited vocabulary he is permitted to use. He just cannot make scintillating stories without a wide selection of words any more than he can build a sophisticated machine with too few parts. Therefore, the first reading material the child has to deal with may not catch *your* imagination. The child, however, is so excited about his new success in reading words that the subject matter, for a while, is not important to him. His ability to use a new learning skill is what catches his imagination at this point, not the subject matter that he is reading.

Some educators have theorized that if the child loved the story, he would make that extra effort to learn to read. I do not find that lack of interest in the story is the problem. Children want to read just as much as they want to learn to ride a bicycle. The child loses interest rapidly, not because of content matter, but because he just cannot memorize those words.

The Silly Stories in the beginning of this program are intellectually limited. Nevertheless, some of the characters are so outrageous the student groans over their stupidity knowing he, himself, is so much smarter. The student who has tasted failure is relieved when he meets a character who seems to perform in a worse manner than he does. In some of the Silly Stories, the animals act like human beings that children like to relate to.

How Can I Get My School Department to Involve Parents in a Reading Program?

It sounds simple enough to ask school administrators to use volunteers to increase the efficiency of a reading program. First, I would suggest that you be an observer in a principal's office for one day to see how many demands are made on this person. If you request the addition of one

---

[19] Walcutt, op. cit., p. 16.

more organizational task, you will be asking the principal to neglect some other area of his or her work.

The coordination of any good program can be a full-time job for one or more persons. Will you back your school committee when budget increases are made?

One community I am familiar with plans to use parent help on a trial basis. The superintendent has his schools involved in a testing program for those students who may be dyslexic. When the students are identified, the parents will be asked to participate actively in the future education of their children. A continuous workshop for parents will be established to give specific directions to these volunteer workers. This superintendent is very enthusiastic about having a manual that can be used by parents.

You can ask your child's teacher, principal, reading resource teacher, or superintendent what plans are being formulated in your community. Volunteer to help.

Should I Have My Child Tutored?

If circumstances are such that you cannot teach your child and you would like to have the child tutored, there are certain areas that should be considered.

Be careful to evaluate in your own mind what you expect from a tutor. You are paying for a service but you cannot expect guarantees. You are not buying a commodity. Remember, you would not expect that a year of one or two hours a week of piano teaching would produce a great pianist, especially if daily practice did not take place. One or two weekly teaching sessions of reading without daily practice will not make a reader.

Some puzzled parents have come to me for tutoring service, stating that the child's teacher would not recommend a tutor for their failing child. Often teachers will make this statement because they have seen parents pay high fees for a year with very limited results. Therefore these teachers sincerely believe tutoring is not the answer to reading problems.

One-to-one teaching of the same method that the child is not responding to in school will not produce much more success than has been experienced in the classroom.

There are tutors who can get John or Betty to read. If you have heard of the marvels of the teacher you would like to have for your child's tutor, you will probably find that this word-of-mouth praise is a good recommendation.

If you feel insecure about your choice, you can ask several parents who have worked with the tutor you are considering what results they have had. If you have no way of learning the names of people the tutor has worked with, you should feel free to ask this teacher to give you names of former students. Also, you can request the tutor to use the Integral Phonics Reading Program.

Tutorial fees for one hour of work may seem exorbitant. Do you realize, however, that a good tutor puts in a minimum of one hour preparatory work for each hour he or she teaches? The child has not succeeded with the available school material, therefore the tutor has to prepare lesson sheets that are tailored for your child.

The tutor is not paid a salary. The work time on the telephone with the parent, or with the child's teacher, and the occasional trip to the school take time. A tutor can easily put in an eight- to twelve-hour day but only be paid for four.

Why Is It Necessary for Parents to Take Over the Teacher's Job?

Parents teach the child skills involving the household, they teach games, and they teach sports, along with many other skills. If parents can reinforce the school program, they should be given the privilege of working with their children in the academic field. These parents would be supplementing the school experience, not trying to take over the teacher's job.

Won't the Slow Process of Learning Words by Analyzing Their Parts
Cause My Child to Be a Slow Reader at a Later Date?

In the past, some educators surmised that slow readers were created by being taught in the beginning grades to puzzle over the parts of the words instead of dealing with words as wholes. There is no research to prove that this process creates slow readers.[20] In fact, many educators state that through their years of teaching, they have concluded that slow readers are those who did not respond well to the whole-word recognition method of teaching. These disabled readers were slowed down in the middle grades because they had no tools to decode the new large words they met.

Neurologists who specialize in the field of language acquisition have felt that immaturity of the nervous system could be the reason why some students have been slow readers.[21] These doctors have also reasoned that the physiological makeup of the slow reader may be different from the fast reader. There are phenomenally rapid runners and others that, no matter how they train, never can compete with the naturally fast performers.

What Is the Procedure the Child Goes Through on a Conscious Level
When He Starts to Learn to Read?

When a child learns to use the letters of the alphabet in relation to the words he must learn, he has to make a conscious effort to recall the sound of these letters. This is an enormous hurdle the beginning reader has to surmount.

Many students become completely confused at this beginning spot. They have proudly mastered the alphabet names of the letters and many can identify the printed letter with its name when it is flashed before them. Then, unfortunately, the child finds he cannot use twenty-one of those letter names in the words he is trying to learn to read. He must associate new sounds for these twenty-one consonants. The letter *s* never sounds like the alphabet *s*. This letter has several sounds. Most often it has a hissing sound, not its name of *s*. (Which is actually *ess!*)

Can you imagine the child's confusion when he finds that all of those consonants never say the names that he has learned. Now the child has to start to learn what sounds are used when he is going to read a word. Right here a conscious effort has to be made. The student cannot remain passive, just receiving stimuli.

[20] Chall, op. cit., p. 113.
[21] Crosby and Liston, op. cit., pp. 52–53.

There are a variety of ways to teach students to connect the image with the sound of each letter. Some students need to use their sense of touch to register the complications of letter symbols. The Integral Phonics Reading Program uses several techniques to establish an image with a specific sound.

Mastering the twenty-one consonant sounds takes a great amount of associative learning. After the child makes the decision about the correct consonant sound, he then has to hold that sound in his mind while he looks at the vowel. In the IPRP, I have the student use the long vowels only over a lengthy period. These long vowels say their alphabet names. The child does not have to try to remember another sound in connection with these letters. He has heard *a, e, i, o, u* for several years at home, on TV, and in kindergarten. The alphabet vowels usually are automatically recalled by the time the student enters first grade. The various sounds of the twenty-one consonants will eventually become automatic, too. For quite a period of time, however, the child has to pull the consonant sound to a conscious level, then he has to combine it with the vowel sound. To finish the work, the student then has to decide what the last consonant sound is and tag that onto the end of the word he has started.

Do you realize how many decisions the child has to make in working with just one word? Luckily, the brain has wondrous power. All these decisions are made in a phenomenally short time even though the beginning attempts by the child seem to drag. Showing the pupil a simplified routine that he must follow each time will produce smooth-flowing progress instead of a confused disaster.

After you have started to teach the lessons, you can reread this section. It will have more meaning for you.

What Do You Mean by Visual Pattern-Sorting?

One of the most important results that will come from teaching the Integral Phonics Reading Program is that the student will acquire the ability to recognize letter patterns rapidly.

The technique for this training starts with the very first lesson. The child learns to reach for the main pattern that tells him what these one-syllable words are. This pattern-sorting is a slow, conscious effort at first. When the child has finished the first book in this program, the patterns he has learned to register on his brain have become quite automatic.

Not only your student but you, yourself, will be looking at words in a new way. You become conscious of patterns like *ow ou, ew oo*. The youngsters pull these out of TV commercials and then are able to say the words immediately — "There is an *ew*, News."

In the later grades, this same skill must be used when getting the main point from a paragraph. This is, of course, a much more complex job. However, the student's early training prepares him for this more complicated task.

The child who has been labeled dyslexic has to go through the pattern-sorting process or he will never learn to read. Many children can become good readers without this emphasis, but they seem to be stimulated by pattern training. They enjoy their spelling lessons (which are usually such a bore), if this puzzling-out takes place. All students benefit by acquiring this skill that helps them so much at a later date.

What Do You Mean by Conscious-Effort Learning?

In conscious associative learning, the pupil *cannot* be a passive receiver of information. The student must make himself select from his mind a familiar piece of knowledge that he can tie to the new information he has to anchor in his memory bank. If he does not associate previously learned material with this new information, there will be no permanent learning experience. Your first reaction may be that this process is too time-consuming; life will pass by before the pupil gets the basics. A surface view of the situation would leave you with the impression that conscious associative learning is cumbersome. Bear in mind, however, that once this procedure is well established as a habit, automation then takes over. When enough patterns are built by a conscious effort, you have created a machine that will work for you.

One of the most exciting experiences a teacher can have is to observe the transition period when the child has built all his conscious effort material into a working mechanism that lets him read automatically. The child now almost teaches himself. He needs the teacher only for guidance in his reading. The teacher now fills in the gaps where the irregularities of our language create booby traps. If the instructor has been able to help the child build good skills, a miracle seems to take place. The child reaches that beautiful point where he no longer crawls, he suddenly walks, walks rapidly, and then he gallops, all in one swoop.

*Should I Be Concerned with the Comprehension Ability
of My Beginning Reading Student?*

When a child is learning to analyze words which will become his reading vocabulary, he is so involved with the analyzing process that comprehension is incidental.

In the recent past, there has been great emphasis put on developing the child's comprehension ability.[22] It is true that poor readers in the upper grades wrestle with comprehension problems. I have found this problem stems mainly from the student's lack of word-decoding skill. The comprehension cannot improve until the reading process becomes automatic, a development that takes place after the conscious analysis skills have been mastered. Therefore, though you want your child to understand the story he is learning to read, this ability will not be perfected until the child actually learns to read accurately.

Can you remember finding the parts of speech in sentences when you had grammar work in school? You were so involved in looking at the structure of your sentence that your comprehension of the subject matter was incidental to the other work you were doing. When a child is learning to read, he will be engrossed in puzzling over the words rather than be concerned with meaning. When the child's reading skills become automatic, he can then concentrate on comprehension.

After (not before) the child has decoded the words in a sentence, reread the sentence to him. He will understand the meaning — that is, if he is listening!

There is a type of student who reads well but has poor comprehension due to attention and conceptual inadequacies. This lack of understanding by the adequate oral reader presents a problem quite different from the problem that frustrates the reader who cannot decode the

22 Chall, op. cit., p. 307.

words. The former student needs intensive remedial work taught by an extremely skilled clinician.

What Types of Basic Readers Are Difficult for the Child Who Has Not Experienced Reading Success?

There seems to be abundant evidence that children with reading difficulties cannot learn to read by the look-and-say method. This method has been given various names, such as the whole-word recognition method, the gestalt approach, or rote memorization of words. Whatever the title is, you must keep reminding yourself that many children do not remember words just by looking at them even though there has been repetitious drill by the classroom teacher or by special tutors.

Many reading publishers rely on the look-and-say method in their basic reading books. The authors of these books will argue that a child cannot learn by any other method until he has memorized by rote a minimum of a hundred and fifty words. For the problem reader, a hundred and fifty words might as well be a hundred and fifty thousand.

These children seem to respond to a simplified phonics reading program which, at first, uses only about ten sight words in order to build sentences. The child can manage to memorize only a small number of sight words. Unfortunately, there is very little agreement on which phonics units should be stressed for the child who has reading difficulties.

Can All Children Become Good Readers?

If your child has natively strong pictorial recall, he or she will become an excellent rapid reader. Probably about one-third of the school population does have this native ability. This is a talent that seems to be inborn but not necessarily related to superior intelligence. The trait appears to be a genetic factor just as is straight or curly hair. This does not mean that the other two-thirds of the population cannot acquire the same kind of skill. One-half of this two-thirds will in time become good readers if exposed to a well-taught phonics system.

Success for the other section of these people will depend entirely upon privilege. If this beginning reader lives in an educationally concerned community, he or she will be programmed to success. Unfortunately, many people are doomed to become discards.

Why Didn't My Other Children Have Reading Problems?

You say, "I do not understand why this child has reading problems. Not one of my other six gave me a bit of trouble." You were just plain lucky. Statistics vary from ten percent to as high as seventy-five percent in stating the numbers of problem readers in this country.[23] Your seventh child just happens to be one who does not respond well to methods that he has been exposed to. He wishes with all his soul he could learn that mass-production school system way.

[23] Crosby and Liston, op. cit., p. 18.

Why Can't My Child Remember the Words?

When you see the Word Lists used in the Integral Phonics Reading Series, you may think that the child can memorize them if they are flashed before him enough times. Many children can memorize the words by repetition and never forget them. Others will store the words for one lesson, but will not be able to transmit them at a later date.

Both types of student have what psychologists call good *short-term* memory.[24] They will quickly memorize the words after they see them a few times. However, the latter group has a *long-term* memory ability different from the former group. These special types of people do not respond to rote learning because their long-term memory functions best by an analysis learning method. These children absolutely must puzzle the words out when learning to read.

Why Does My Child Memorize Accurately Only to Forget the Material the Next Day?

The intricacies of how we memorize fills volumes. In spite of all these volumes, the scientist still cautions the layman that precious little is known about how the brain actually stores knowledge.

Observations do tell us that retention of information can be improved by a variety of techniques. Human beings seem to have various abilities for memory retention. When one memorizes digits to dial the telephone, he remembers just long enough to dial the number. If he wants to store that number in his mind for later use, he has to develop a technique for anchoring the number. This procedure may or may not be successful depending upon many factors. Schoolwork for the child is similar to the dialing procedure. Much of the time the student learns for the moment but has not acquired techniques to retain information permanently.

The physiological or neurological development of the individual has a great bearing on the facility that each individual has in coping with memory work. Many youngsters may not be ready at target dates to perform specific memory skills any more than a young growing child is ready to be an Olympic athlete.

Why Does My Child Mouth the Words?

When a child begins to read, he will often form the words in his mouth with a very noticeable motion. Teachers used to frown upon this action, thinking its performance would be detrimental to the child's later reading rate. Enlightened teachers have come to realize that the mouthing of words at the beginning stages is quite normal for many children. Youngsters soon drop the habit when the decoding process becomes automatic. Those students who seem to continue the mouthing procedure an unusually long time do so because they are in need of individualized help.

Some students will mouth the word, then whisper it to themselves correctly and proceed

24 Hunter, op. cit., p. 63.

orally to mispronounce it. This is not an abnormal performance but is part of normal neurological growth for that child. If he is shamed, corrected impatiently, and not encouraged, you can be assured that emotional struggles will soon follow. (See the appendix.)

Will Word Recognition Ever Become Automatic for My Child?

After you see the painful struggle these youngsters go through to analyze words, you will question whether the words can ever be anchored automatically. The struggle is part of the neurological development of the child. Just remember that you were not impatient when you let your child go through the struggle of learning to crawl. Eventually he was scampering all over the place. You will see a similar process take place while the child works through the process of decoding words, culminating in automatic recall; that is, if you do not get irritated while he works through the lessons.

Why Does My Child Rebel When I Try to Work with Him?

You may have developed a full-blown personality clash. It might be better for some other member of the family to work with the child. Another alternative is to exchange with a neighbor's child. You all may have more patience if you are not emotionally involved. Maybe working with your child in this program will be the beginning of a new relationship. When you follow the directives in this book, you may discover what has been triggering previous clashes.

If you have met rebellion while trying to drill schoolwork on previous occasions, the upheaval could have been caused by the material you both had to work with. If the child could not do the work well in the classroom, one-to-one work at home with the same system does not assure any more success. The materials and method did not fit your child's learning pattern. The child is just as frustrated and just as unsuccessful at home as he was in the classroom. He, however, has had the good manners not to take his frustrations out on the school personnel. When he gets home, he has to let off steam. The explosions are directed at the person who works with him on the home front.

A miserable, irritating communication system may have been building. Explain this whole situation to your child. State that with a new set of materials, a new method, and a new understanding you should be able to work together.

Keep in mind that you will have to develop more patience than you expect from your child. When your youngster reverts back to old forms of rebellion, you will have to state *without irritation* that you know he is impatient but he has got to give himself a fair trial without all the fussing. No rewards if he starts to find excuses why he does not want to work.

Do *not* find fault. Do *not* criticize mistakes. Do *not* accuse your pupil of not trying. Find some positive action for compliments. You really can find something he does right. Maybe at first it will be nothing more than the fact you like the way he holds the book! Each lesson should bring about several complimentary statements. Even if you have to ask for four corrections while struggling on *one* word, the final success should be praised.

You may be happily surprised to see how cooperative your child can be. I have had parents offer to pay me more as long as they do not have to work with their child. These very parents have eventually, to their surprise, become highly successful teachers for their own youngsters.

Should My Child Be Rewarded for Success?

Yes, your child should be rewarded when he reaches set goals. For a period of time, gold stars or special privileges for goal accomplishments were frowned upon by educators. Rewards are now considered respectable again. In fact, some educational journals have advertisements for prize kits, all kinds of little trinkets, to surprise the students when they reach an established goal. (Technical term: "extrinsic reward"!)

There are still some teachers who feel setting goals for the child creates too much pressure. There are other teachers who have found that, in the early grades, the child has not matured to the point where the sense of accomplishment is a reward in itself. The young student seems to want someone to help him set goals which, when met, will have some special reward.

I hang a large sheet of paper on the wall. (A large paper bag slit down the side and bottom, then opened, can be used for this poster.) A round world is drawn in the lower left-hand corner and a moon at the top right-hand corner. At intervals I paste (flour-and-water paste is easiest) small individual squares on the road to the moon. Each square represents one phonic integral. As he progresses, the child cuts out a paper spaceship he has drawn and pins it on each square. I make a star at a specific spot to represent prize day (every two weeks or so).

The prizes I have awarded have been a little car, a truck, a doll's dish set, or a ball, etc. (I have made clothes for dolls or G.I. Joes.) I know that budget-wise this is not possible in many households. Therefore, rewards can be a special trip to the park, staying up an hour later on a Friday night, no dishes to do some night, special dessert for the whole family (the child likes giving this to his family and the family shows the child more appreciation).

If you have a hyperactive child, it would be worthwhile for you to read about the techniques used for a merit system that the behavior modification psychologists have developed. The extremely active child often cannot wait for long-range rewards. Special plans should be created for this youngster.

Instead of a trip to the moon, you can have a race track, or sports event. Your child will offer many ideas. The poster can represent steps for each new unit. The days of the week can be charted on another paper so that the child can make a cross with his colored pen in each section to show he has completed his daily review session. You can tell your child you will put a check in the daily space with another colored pen if he has been ready on time for his lesson and has not fussed about having to work each day. You can give his prize a day earlier if he has your checkmark each day. Do not expect to have him act perfectly. However, do not reward him if he has been unreasonable. Do not confuse apathy with honest temporary inability. There are days when the child will not do as well as on other days. If you show impatience, the child literally blocks and *cannot* do the work well. Much of the work at first seems simple to you, but it will not be easy for the child. Just keep repeating the Seven Special Steps described in the lessons and show some humor. Eventually, the child relaxes and does well.

Isn't a Reward System Really a Form of Bribery?

There is a fine line at some point between when we use the term "reward" and when we use the term "bribery." The original meaning of bribery suggests the use of a reward to promote a corrupt act. Therefore, can you call the reward system a form of bribery? You are not giving a reward to encourage your child to do something corrupt. The prize is for work well done. You are motivating this student to set goals for himself.

What about the argument that the child will expect a reward for every accomplishment? Is this so bad? Can you honestly think of anything that is done in life that is not accomplished for the sake of reward, whether it be material reward or emotional gratification? You often say to your child, "You cannot go out to play until you have made your bed." Is this bribery?

You can teach your student to set up his own reward system. He can find his own prizes. Often a student will say, "I can't take a bite of that cookie until I have read two full sentences." Eventually the goal is set for full paragraphs before he rewards himself.

If My Child Becomes a Good Reader, Will This Mean
He Will Be a Good Speller?

Good reading ability will not automatically guarantee adequate spelling performance. Each skill is basically quite different. Very few educators have examined the differences in mechanics involved in these two areas.

A skilled athletic coach knows exactly what body mechanisms have to be trained for specific sports. It seems quite obvious that a golfer and a wrestler use different body mechanics. The disparities between the art of reading and the art of spelling are not so evident.

The main steps used when learning to read start with the process of looking at a printed page, seeking patterns within the word, then analyzing the word by means of acquired knowledge, and continuing by registering the whole word to bring forth the word's meaning in relation to previously acquired knowledge. Finally, the reader must reach out to the next word while carrying the meaning of the sentence at the same time. This whole process involves the eye-to-brain pathway or, if one is blind, touch instead of sight is tapped.

The art of spelling requires more circuitous processes plus the use of entirely different neurological pathways compared to the act of reading. The act of spelling can be divided into two broad categories. One procedure involves a list of words that the student hopes to memorize in order to pass a spelling test. The other spelling process takes place during letter-writing or report-writing.

The student uses his reading skill when he tries to memorize spelling words. At test time the student has to receive the sound accurately and transpose that sound into one of the complex reading patterns that he has to recall and visualize. Then he has to be able to transmit this pattern to the paper. At one point, a process that is the reverse of reading must be accomplished. Reversal procedures are extremely confusing tasks for many people. The concluding action calls for finger-pencil coordination as well as decision-making concerning the drawing of special shapes for each letter. Did you ever realize what an amazing phenomenon you have mastered?

Then, to make the whole subject more confusing, you have to realize that using spelling skill in report-writing is much more complex than the spelling and testing experience.

Complicated thought organizing has to take place before the words can be put down. Sentence structure must be considered and constantly held in mind while the hand and mind must coordinate decision-making with regard to the right configuration for individual letters, words, and phrases. The sequence of the letters has to be correctly recalled for each specific word. These are a few of the details to be considered before the final step of actually putting pencil to paper. Success in spelling is truly a complicated set of mental and physical gymnastics.

TWO:
FOR THOSE USING
THE INTEGRAL PHONICS
READING PROGRAM

*If the Teacher Decides He or She Would Like to Use the Integral Phonics
Reading Program, Would the System Be Practical in a Large Classroom?*

The IPRP has already been used by classroom teachers. When the students I tutor are checked for progress by their teachers, the student reads from the IPRP. These teachers have asked if they could use the material.

An adult volunteers to type the stories on carbons that can be run through a duplicating machine. I have had glowing reports of success from teachers who have used my materials.

There are certain areas in which a teacher cannot give the time that you can as a parent. Children who have perceptual problems (and there are many) need one-to-one attention when they first struggle with the consonant and long-vowel blending. Here is the place where you can give help that is not feasible in a large classroom.

*Does My Child Do the School Homework While I Am
Teaching the Integral Phonics Reading Program?*

Teachers often send home a list of words or a book the child has failed to manage in school. The parent is asked to drill the material into the child. This method has not worked in school and probably does not work at home.

Now is the time to have a visit with the teacher, not at a PTA meeting. Set a date at the teacher's convenience. (I know you are working but you can keep doctors' appointments. This meeting is just as important.)

WARNING: Tread lightly, teachers are human. They can feel just as threatened as you do when you have more work than you can manage to do well. Make a point of being friendly no matter how angry you may feel about your child's reading problems. You do not like to take directives from an irritating boss. The teacher will not respond to an annoyed tone of voice. Explain to the teacher you have great sympathy for his or her lot. Compliment this teacher for what he or she has done well, or for his or her effort in trying.

Explain to the teacher you have been advised to try a new program (my book) which demands daily homework. You would appreciate Johnny's being excused from his present school homework. Tell the teacher you may not be able to succeed (but you will!), and if you feel you do not plan to continue the program you will report this immediately. Also assure the teacher you are not asking to have the child excused from his daily work *in* school.

. The teacher may protest that the student will become confused. Say that you are willing to take that risk and that you sincerely hope this will not happen. (It won't.) Remember, your optimistic attitude will rub off on the teacher as well as the child.

(After starting the Integral Phonics Reading Program with students, we check in three weeks' time with the teachers. We have yet to hear a teacher say there had been no improvement in the child's schoolwork, even when there had been little at this point in the home program that could have been integrated into the schoolwork. The child's home success relaxes him enough so that he approaches his daily work with a new attitude.)

Do I Have to Buy Gadgets for this Program?

MINIMUM EQUIPMENT: This book and two pencils.
EXTRAS IF POSSIBLE: Plain paper, lined paper, scissors, crayons, or preferably, a set of colored, felt-tip pens (not the broad markers).

Junk mail makes good paper on the nonprinted side. Save any gummed labels or stamps and the envelopes that come in unsolicited mail. The child likes to put the stamps on his papers.

If you have an old briefcase or a box to decorate, the equipment can be kept in this container. *Never* borrow it for other work. It gets lost. Be firm about this rule. The child takes pride in his "office" equipment. The materials are his and *no one* in the family should be allowed to borrow them. Here is something for his very own he does not have to share. This can be a good family lesson in property rights. You do not share your gold ring with the neighbor or the children. Your child's property is as dear to him as your gold ring is to you.

How Much Time Will I Have to Give to This Program?

There is no magic that will build "instant" readers. Any skill takes time to learn. However, you will see amazing progress if you can spend *fifteen minutes* twice a day or one-half an hour once a day, five days a week for three months. There is one big *if.* You will meet success in that time *if* you stick to this routine. Skipping a few days here and there will handicap your reader. Two hours of grind for missed days will spell disaster. It will not be the equivalent of four half-hour sessions or eight fifteen-minute periods.

If you are a parent teaching your child, you are the one who has to set the pace. You should decide you want to do this as a stimulating project for your child. Do *not* start if you are going to resent the effort. Do *not* expect the child to remind you of the schedule. You constantly have to encourage and support him. You must state unemotionally that it is time for the lesson and that you are not going to accept excuses. Your child finds out he might as well cooperate. The parents who have tested this program for me have not run into uncooperative attitudes. The children seem so relieved to find they can succeed that they work very hard.

One other point — it is wise to set aside a specific time each day when your child is not hungry or too tired. Juice and crackers just before starting helps. Eating breakfast fifteen minutes earlier before the school day starts followed by a lesson is a good schedule for many children, as is fifteen minutes directly after the night meal. (The dishes can wait.) This may seem rough for the working parent or inconvenient for the cocktail group, but the maternal or paternal instinct can overcome obstacles. If you complete this program, you will find the child needs very little reading help in the later grades.

If I Teach My Child the Integral Phonics Reading Program,
When Will I Begin to Get Some Insight about My Child's Learning Pattern?

You will probably begin to realize within a few lessons what mechanics are involved in order to tap your child's learning pattern. By the time you have covered parts 1 and 2 of the lessons, you will have a true appreciation of the complicated process reading really is. You will see how difficult it is to absorb large numbers of words for instant recall. Lucky are those who can look at something and then, without conscious effort, recall the detail. Often these same people wish they had had the disciplined training that is required by the people who must analyze before a permanent memory bank is acquired. This conscious organized learning process has to be used by all people eventually.

Will the Teacher Cooperate with Me While I Am Working
with the Integral Phonics Reading Program?

It depends upon the teacher whether he or she will cooperate with your new venture. Some teachers will welcome being introduced to the Integral Phonics Reading Program. They will congratulate you for taking the initiative in helping to correct a problem. Another teacher may be so relieved that she has one less program to send home, she will eagerly accept your plan.

There will be some teachers who will be opposed to anything that does not follow their ritual. They may describe to you all the dire consequences that will result if you deviate from the norm. If you have decided to try the program, you have to show your strength and take a positive approach in a friendly way. You will not change the attitude of rigid teachers. You have to respect your own judgment and take your own road. You know your child better than anyone else. Remember, if your child is not reading well, you will not compound the problem by trying another method. He certainly will not be any worse off than he is, and if you have patience and persevere, you will be the one who brings success to your child.

If I Make Mistakes, Will My Child Lose Respect for Me?

When some parents start teaching their children, the first attempt may be awkward. The student senses his parent's insecurity. Your child may state that he is not going to work with someone who is so slow or so stupid. The immediate reaction from the parents is that their child does not respect them. Tempers flare.

You can avoid this situation by explaining to the child at the beginning that you are a new teacher and that when anyone starts a new adventure, mistakes are made. Adults make mistakes just like children. We can all try to learn together. In the future, we are not going to blame each other for mistakes. The child may ask why he has been yelled at in the past. (This will give you an idea of how you may have been frustrating your youngster!) You can say that just because you are grown up does not mean you know how to do everything perfectly. You, too, are learning.

Many adults have been conditioned to believe that making a mistake is a sign of weakness. They may soon find that admitting mistakes commands respect, not disrespect.

How Can I Tell Whether My Child Does Not Understand or Whether He Does Not Listen?

Some students have a very short attention span. Their thoughts tend to drift from one exciting idea to another. You cannot be sure the child really is tuned in to what you feel is important information. These students often may not have developed physiologically and neurologically as rapidly as their peers.

Here you meet the situation that can be compared to that point in time when one child may start to walk later than the neighbor's child. The parents of the delayed walker may have a twinge of apprehension which is soon alleviated when their child starts catching up with his neighbor.

When our child's attention span is not highly developed by the time he is in school, however, we, as well as the teacher, become extremely apprehensive. The child is blamed for not trying. Rarely do we question whether the child's nervous system has developed enough to allow him to direct his interest to the task at hand for a reasonable length of time.

The child soon learns to feel he is less than adequate. He escapes his guilt feeling by tuning out. This mechanism complicates the developmental growth. Daydreaming becomes highly refined.

You may find that your child is very well behaved, he just does not listen. When you explain a new concept, he seems to be attentive but he does not comprehend. You have to realize your child is just not capable of listening at that moment.

If this child is scolded or reprimanded, he becomes so self-conscious his efforts become fruitless because he keeps saying to himself, "I must listen, I must listen." By this time the information has not been heard because the child has tried so hard to listen!

If you find your child has blocked, stop the type of work you are doing. Say to the child, in a patient voice, "I think you are trying too hard. Let's work with something else." Choose a review area he has done well in the past. With patience you will find your child will respond.

He will have fewer lapses if you learn to switch material at the appropriate moment. As you progress, you will find a new way to catch his attention.

Why Are There No Suffixes on the One-Syllable Words in the First Few Silly Stories?

Putting *s, ed,* or *ing* on a word adds a tremendous burden to the beginning reader. This addition may seem very simple to you but you have forgotten the frustrations you had when you began to read.

It is a neurological miracle that the eye and the brain are able to coordinate to allow for the discrimination of word patterns. It takes several sessions for the child to find similarities in words with such patterns as the consonant-vowel-consonant-silent *e* pattern (*bake, cake, take,* etc.). Turn to the Word List in Lesson 26 with long *a.* You can look at that page and soon see the word pattern. The beginning reader just sees a bunch of words, pretty confusing words at that. Until the student can handle this pattern, there is no point in adding the misery of word endings.

In the IPRP, these suffixes are not added until the child is ready. Then these ending letters are underlined so that the child can see the original pattern of the word; he can blank out the last letter or letters while he wrestles with the main part (baked) (bakes). The suffix *ing* is not used as such until the child is well into the decoding process.

Why Isn't the Student Who Uses the Integral Phonics Reading Program Trained to Use the Context of the Sentence to Find Clues to Decode the Words?

Some basic reading programs expect the student to be able to guess what a word is if he has been able to read the rest of the words in the sentence. This system may work well for some, but for those who are not blessed with a strong visual memory this procedure does nothing but train the child in guessing games.

The Integral Phonics Reading Program was originally designed to help the pupil who had not succeeded in reading. This type of student has to use reliable mechanical procedures for each word he meets. He cannot afford the luxury of guessing, a snare that diverts many students into poor work habits.[1]

The student who cannot process the words he sees into a memory bank in his brain must consciously analyze each word in a systematic way. When the child uses this analyzing process, his oral reading may sound awkward for several weeks or months. If the teacher remains patient, he or she will be rewarded. Eventually the process does become automatic; the student *does* reach that point where he reads smoothly. He, also, has learned a solid decoding process that will continue to work for him when he meets complex words in the upper grades.

Phonic patterns are the tools the student uses to analyze (decode) the words. These are the tools that all students have to use when learning to spell. The child who is not endowed with

[1] Helen R. Rowe, "The Whole-Word and Word-Guessing Fallacy," in Charles C. Walcutt, ed., *Tomorrow's Illiterates: The State of Reading Instruction Today* (Boston: Little, Brown, 1961), pp. 103–104.

a strong visual aptitude cannot possibly spell without the conscious effort involved in working with phonic integrals.

Why Do the Silly Stories in the Integral Phonics Reading Program Introduce Words or Situations Some Children Would Not Have Met?

The Silly Stories are designed to use words the student can analyze with his new skills. Some of the words and situations may be unfamiliar to the student. They have been used purposely to create discussion which will lead to exposure to new knowledge.

The child who lives in the city, whether it be the ghetto or the privileged areas, will meet small-town situations that he has not experienced. And in reverse, some of the Silly Stories include information that will be novel to the small-town student. This gives all types of students new insights.

The child may never have heard or used several of the words. The words happen to fit a phonics pattern and are good for discussions of what they mean. This is vocabulary-building exposure.

Why Are There No Pictures in the Integral Phonics Reading Series?

Bright youngsters who are not sight readers learn to use the pictures as part of a guessing game. They are successful enough in the maneuver so that they may bluff through testing only to meet disaster as time passes. With no pictures to distract the student, he finds he has to rely on his newfound skills.[2]

Usually the child likes to draw his own picture about the story after he has read it. Do *not* correct his drawing. It may look miserable to you and he may be dissatisfied with it. Just tell your child it is a fun picture and you like it the way it is.

Aren't the Sentences in the Silly Stories Rather Long for Beginning Readers?

Long sentences are not harder to manage than short ones.[3] The child's comprehension of the major information in the sentences will not be good when he first begins to read. He has to concentrate so hard on word analysis that comprehension is forfeited. Therefore it is wise to reread aloud the sentence or the paragraph *after* the child has finished. This stimulates the student to read on to find what will happen to the characters in the story.

Most students need to continue as long as possible along one line. Having to jump to the next line is not easy for the beginning reader.

I do not use quotation marks in the Silly Stories until the child is well established. The clutter of these marks is very distracting to many students. You want your student to concen-

[2] Walcutt, op. cit., pp. 20–21.
[3] Lloyd W. Goos, "Linguistics for the Dyslexic," in John Money, ed., *The Disabled Reader* (Baltimore: Johns Hopkins Press, 1966), p. 87.

trate on letter patterns. If there are many quotation marks, they clutter the peripheral vision, hampering concentration on specific elements of the word.

Why Aren't Capital Letters Taught Before the Lowercase Form in the IPRP?

If you are teaching a piece of information to the student that he will need for future use, it is important to correlate the lesson with direct usage of the information. If capital letter formations are taught in isolation from their function, many students become confused about when to use capitals and when to use lowercase letters. This situation occurs if factual information is taught in a vacuum. An example of this problem takes place during the weekly spelling lessons. Lists of words are studied and memorized for perfect testing, only to be lost for future use. Asking the student to memorize the shapes of capital letters when he does not have to use them falls into the category of a futility exercise. I start the capital letter orientation at the time the student has to use the big letters for the beginning of his first printed sentences.

What Do I Do if My Student Needs More Reading Material for One of the Phonic Integrals Presented in This Book?

You may be able to create your own Silly Stories for your student by using the reading lists. If you do not feel capable of this task, you will, with a little practice, be able to compose and type a list of individual Silly Sentences using the specific integral that is troubling your student. If you are using the IPRP in the classroom you, of course, will need the extra stories.

When Can I Start to Teach This Program?

You can start any time of the year, any time of the week, and any time of the day. Your first lesson may seem to be disorganized. Within a few sessions, you will discover ways to overcome awkward gaps. Keep your sense of humor; encourage your student to laugh over the mistakes both of you make. Read the following fifteen hints; you may want to refer to them often. Enjoy yourself.

Fifteen Hints for the Teacher and Parent

1. Each word list and its accompanying story should be read at least three or four times. (Only once at each sitting.)
2. The student should reread the lessons enough so that they become easier each time.
3. Some students need learning sessions twice a day. As the pupil progresses, one session each day may be enough.
4. The student should analyze the words in each lesson.

5. If he is reading from memory instead of really looking at the words, go to the next lesson immediately. Return at a later time to review.

6. If you are teaching your child before he is of school age, you may find the youngster has a beautiful rote memory ability. For this type of child, do not demand complete analysis of each word after he has anchored the word.

7. Do make sure the rote memory type of child can decode. He can learn this process through the spelling lessons.

8. The child should be encouraged to make pictures to illustrate any of the Silly Stories. Let the child draw whatever he wishes. Compliment, do not criticize, his work. Do not try to show him how to improve some image in his picture unless he asks you for help. Whatever he draws is valid for his development. If the child is not succeeding too well in school, he is frustrated enough. Trying to get your child to draw in a photographic way will not help him in his academic work. Therefore, let him have the drawing sessions as an outlet of relaxation. .

9. Never, never, never tell your student he is stupid. You may think he is not trying, but he may be trying too hard. If he does seem to be giving you a hard time, your getting angry and calling him stupid will not cure the problem. (If you make a mistake, does a screaming person make you want to correct your error? Usually anger breeds anger.)

10. If the child has struggled very hard over the words in a sentence, it is wise for you to reread the sentence aloud for him so that he may review the meaning. The child may want to discuss the silly situations in the stories.

11. Do not be surprised when your child seems to whisper the word correctly to himself but pronounces it wrong. It takes a long time to make everything come out even. (See the question, Why Does My Child Mouth the Words?)

12. If the student is having trouble decoding the word, do not read it for him. Be sure he works through the Seven Special Steps.

13. Laugh about mistakes.

14. Tell your student he has to make his brain stop playing tricks on him!

15. Praise, praise, praise.

2

Daily Lessons

SEVEN SPECIAL STEPS

(To be used in each lesson)

Note to parent-teacher: Vowels are: *a, e, i, o, u* and sometimes *y*. Consonants are the other twenty-one letters of the alphabet.

1. Teacher points to the word with a pencil. (The finger is too large.) Child looks at the word and counts the vowels, "First vowel, second vowel."
2. Child crosses second vowel out (with pencil to make his eyes blank out the silent second vowel).*
3. Ask the child to repeat aloud that first vowel sound, loud and long.
4. Ask the child to repeat the first letter sound. Now ask him to blend that first letter (consonant) with the long-vowel sound. *Example: so* in the word *soap.*
5. If wrong, ask the child to repeat aloud step 3. Continue with step 4. Keep repeating steps 3 and 4 until there is success. If the child has no success after several attempts, the teacher should repeat aloud steps 3 and 4.
6. Child then repeats corrected sound.
7. Child finally adds last consonant sound and *repeats* the whole word aloud.

* Soon the child will not need to cross out the second vowel with his pencil. Keep reminding him to blank out in his mind that silent second vowel.

Copy this sheet onto a separate paper to be available for each lesson.

NOTE: I cannot stress strongly enough the importance of following the Seven Special Steps procedure. If you are using this book for a student with a learning disability, you probably will find that you need to spend a greater number of days on each lesson than you would for a pupil who just needs a minimal amount of remedial help.

That student who is in trouble will have acquired some bad habits that have to be changed before much progress is made. If he has been exposed to the look-and-say method and has not succeeded, he will have become skillful at guessing. Keep telling him that guessing days are over. You now want him to look carefully at the word and find the first vowel that says its name. The dyslexic student often cannot accomplish step 4. For him you point your pencil to the long vowel again and have him repeat it aloud. Then you repeat it, dragging the sound out. Ask him to repeat that vowel again, dragging it out loud and long. Then he is to complete step 4.

The student who has this blending problem is helped if you have him focus on the word while you quickly cover the last two letters with a card. (Not your finger, it is too large.)

INTRODUCTORY LESSON

A minimum of words that cannot be sounded out phonetically will be used where they are needed to make complete sentences. A variety of ways are suggested to help the child anchor these irregular words. They will be discussed in the Extra Words section of the lessons. In many basic reading programs an entire body of these words has to be taught on the look-and-say basis before the student starts decoding (analyzing) with phonics. These sight words are the traps that often prevent students from meeting reading success. That is why so few are used in the Integral Phonics Reading Program.

The Phonics section of each lesson gives directions for analyzing words. The first phonic integral introduced is the long *o* followed by *a*. If you look at Lesson 13, you will see that most one-syllable long-vowel words come in two patterns. These words always have two vowels, the first one makes the sound of its alphabet name, the second one is silent.

The group of *ōa* words in Lesson 3 have what I call the peanut butter and jelly word pattern. The consonants are the slices of bread, the first vowel is crunchy peanut butter that you can hear, and the silent vowel is the jelly. The other type of long-vowel words is the layer-cake pattern (or silent *e* words) which will be described later.

In the introduction, I stated that this book is designed for students who have already learned to connect the sound of the letters with their printed symbol. However, a brief review of the sight and sound of the consonants is given.

The directives for the first few lessons seem lengthy. If you follow them carefully, you will have very little introductory material to read in later lessons.

The following information is for the student who may have left-right directional confusion.

Explain to the new reader how to hold a book. The pages he will be turning are right near the side he uses the most, his right side. Tell your left-hander the open side of the book will be next to that hand he does not like to use when he eats.

Now open the book to the page where the story starts. (You can explain the table of contents and title page later. Your child wants to get right down to business.) Show the student you read across the page. You are really hiding in the binding where the book is sewed together. You now come out and walk across the page to the opposite side. When you come to the last word on that line, you race back into the binding to get ready to start the next line. Many children already have this sequence anchored. There are other children who still hesitate about where to start and how to continue.

ONE: LONG VOWELS

LESSON 1

Phonics: Letters *o, a, c, g*

Many students have difficulty with the varied styles of type in reading books. When the child has acquired some skill in decoding words, he or she will adjust to the changes. You, as his teacher, should compare the print in various books. Examine the *a* and the *g*. Your student will not be forming these letters in the traditional style used in most books. The shape of these letters in his reading material will coincide with his own printing until he is able to make the adjustment of recognizing the more complicated configuration of *a* and *g*. Also, the letter *t* will not have a tail on it in the reading lessons until the student is ready for the change.

If you do not have half-inch-lined paper, make twelve lines one-half inch apart on plain paper. Then rule dotted lines, with a red fine ballpoint pen, across alternate spaces. (Have the student skip every other line when he writes so he will not jam letters together.) Draw lines vertically a quarter of an inch apart. Put dots on the vertical lines as indicated in the illustration.

The dot is the starting point for right-handed and left-handed students. Tell your student he is going to learn about words that have two special vowels. First he will practice making a few *o*'s. Direct the child to place his pencil on the dot. He then pushes the pencil around the square. He is to start on the dot and make his pencil go in the direction of his other hand. On the way he will greet his hand that holds the paper in the upper left corner by saying, "Hi, hand." (The left-hander will have his free hand in the right corner. He will say, "Bye, hand.")

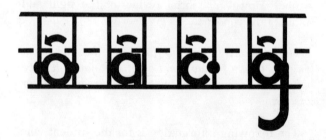

This exercise establishes direction that will be uniform. Many students have trouble drawing letters because no routine starting direction has been learned.

Have the child make several *o*'s. (Do not expect perfection.) Encourage the child to stay within each box and meet the sides. Usually the child is taught to use a full-line space to form big letters, the theory being that small children have poor finger coordination for fine detail work. My students have found letter formation in the big size to be more difficult than in the smaller size.

Tell your child this letter *o* is round and open, forming a shape just like his lips do when he says the letter *o* clearly. (Have him form his lips into a round *o* and repeat the sound.) Now explain that *o* is going to invite a friend to stand beside him. The *o* makes his friend stand second in line and tells him he cannot make any noise. He must be silent. Because *o* is first in line, he will have first chance to say his name. He speaks out loud his alphabet name of *o*. His silent friend's name is *a*. The letter *a* is shaped just like *o* but he leans on a stick. There he is, *a*, leaning on a stick but he must not speak. (Teacher prints *a*.)

Have the student make the *o* shape by starting on the dot, marching in the same direction as before; then have your student lean a straight line on the spot where he joined the circle. The student is to make several *a*'s. Now have him start a new line. He is to print the letter *o* and place *o*'s silent friend *a* beside *o*. Have him make three sets of *oa*. State that *o* is first in line and he shouts his name. Point to *o*, ask the student what name does the letter say. (Answer, *o*.) Poor *a* cannot speak.

Now explain that *o* can act like crunchy peanut butter and *a* will be jelly. Your student will soon be able to make quite a few words using *oa* in the middle. The two letters *o* and *a* are called vowels, such a funny name. Print the word *vowels* on an envelope. Cut up some paper to make 1″ × 2″ cards. Print *o* on one card and *a* on another. Have your student put the letters in the vowel envelope. Keep reminding him about *o* and *a* being vowels.

With two more letters your student will have enough letters to make words. The letter *c* starts on the red dot just like *o*; it goes in the same direction but does not close up. Demonstrate, then have him make *c*. (When *c* is the first letter in a word, this alphabet letter changes its sound. When your student starts reading words with hard *c*, give him the sound.)

There is still another letter that circles in the same direction as that original *o*. (Reinforcement and repetition of shape and direction.) This new letter is **g**. Show your student how you make the *o* and then pull down, making a monkey's tail. The tail curl goes over and up to say, "Hi, hand." This **g** has his soft-sounding alphabet name but when he stands beside *oa* he changes that **g** sound to another sound.

If your student is learning the identification of these letters and their sounds for the first time, you can stop your lesson now. The child who has had exposure to these letters before may want to continue to the next lesson.

LESSON 2

Phonics: The letter *t*

Have paper with dotted lines ready ahead of time. Do not make your child sit around while you are fixing the paper. For review ask your student to print the letters o, a, c, and g. Now you will show your student how to make the letter t. It is a straight line down the middle of the block on his paper with an added cross line. (Copy the dots as in the illustration.)

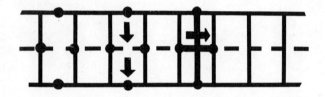

Your student has to connect the dots in the following sequence (always insist he follow the sequence you are building. This is to prevent letter reversals). Start the letter t at the top line, connect at the bottom. Cross from left to right (same direction for a lefty).

Explain that when he sees the letter in a word, the alphabet name changes. Give the sound. Have him give the *sound* of several *t*'s in a row, *ttttttttt* (rapidly). Can he feel the tickle on his lips? (This exercise is important because some people have trouble distinguishing between the sound of *d* and *t* at the end of a word. The dyslexic child often cannot make the distinction. In the next lesson the difference in the *t* and *d* sounds will be discussed.)

Now your child can work with two words. On the 1″ × 2″ paper (we will call them cards in the future) carefully print **coat** on one piece and **goat** on another.

The fun begins, or maybe the frustration. Some children will know the words by sight from school or TV. Those who do not must follow the Seven Special Steps, which appear after this lesson. First, ask which vowel is going to talk in the word **goat**. Lightly cross out a. Point to o. Have the student say the vowel o aloud. Then ask him for the hard sound of g. Can he combine g with o? If he can say **go**, then can he add the sound of *t*?

This procedure sounds simple and it is easy for some students. The dyslexic person will just be beginning his struggles. Be sure to be enthusiastic with each letter success. When the student makes a mistake, tell him his brain is playing tricks on him. He has to slow down and think carefully. Point to the vowel, have him repeat it, dragging it out as *ooooooooooo*. Then point to g and ask him to add hard g to o. Take a card and block off the at (or **goat**) until he can say the sound. Do NOT say it for him. Keep pointing to the vowel, tell him to say this vowel loud and long. Then point to g and have him combine the two letters.

Some students will say *o* perfectly then proceed to say *ga, gi, ge, or* anything but *go*. Do *not* repeat the sound for him. This procedure of the Seven Special Steps, allowing the student to struggle with the blending, is the most important point in the whole program. You must follow this process every time you give the student a new vowel integral.

The blending struggle strengthens the brain pathways needed for decoding words. If you have the patience to follow these instructions, you will be rewarded beyond measure when your child eventually begins to perform the process automatically.

Your student can finish the lesson by decoding the word *coat* using the same mechanics.

LESSON 3

Phonics: The letter *d* and long *o* in *oa*

Review by asking your student to print the letters he has learned. The next letter is to be *d*. This starts just like *o* but pushes a stick line up. Then the pencil comes down to the bottom line. Once again you are reinforcing a basic structure using one type of direction. The letter *d* does not use its alphabet name (which is really *dee*). The sound of *d* is like the first sound in the word *duck*. (Do not print this word for him to see. However, you can make a picture of a duck from the letter *d*. See illustration.) Have your pupil repeat the sound.

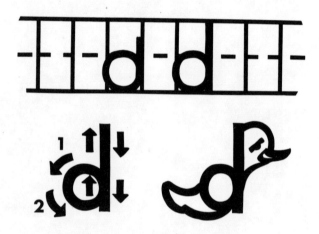

Do not be impatient if your child makes mistakes or does not understand what you mean. It all seems easy to you but you have forgotten how difficult the process was when you were learning. If he is having trouble, he is probably trying too hard. Your child does want to please you. He will eventually stop his blocking if you are relaxed. Just reassure him that the work is difficult, but his mind will soon be working well for him.

Ask your pupil to listen to the word *toad*. Ask what vowel he hears, then what first letter he hears. Have him print what he has repeated, which will be *tō*. He may remember to add *a*. If he does not, ask what vowel friend wants to stay with *o*. (Maybe he cannot remember. Then tell him that *o* likes his friend who has his same shape but leans on a stick — the letter *a*.) Now repeat the word *toad*. Ask what letter this word ends in. Can he finish printing the word?

You print the word *toad* on a paper slip. Can he

read it? Take out the other slips of paper that have *goat* and *coat*. Mix the words up. Can he read them?

This will be so easy for some students that you may wonder why all the detail. You are building a procedure that is important.

Some students have difficulty hearing the difference between the *t* and the *d*. Ask your pupil to repeat the lip-tickling *t* several times: *ttttttttttt*. Then have him repeat *d*. If he makes a good strong sound of *d* in his throat, he can feel the vibrations on the glands each side of his Adam's apple. The letter *t* has a crossbar like the line he makes for a mouth when he makes a face picture,

that line that tickles on his lips when he says the letter *t*. The letter *d* is *d*own *d*eep in the round hole in the throat.

At last your student is ready to read the Silly Sentences. He will read the underlined words; you will fill in the others. (He may know the other words by sight. An adult usually cannot understand why the tiny words can be misread. For the troubled reader, the two-letter words look too much alike. Until the student can consistently associate a specific sound with a specific letter shape, he will not be able to store an accurate image that can be recalled correctly at a later date. This feat is extremely difficult for the dyslexic.)

Use the Seven Special Steps to help your pupil decode his *oa* words.

The student may begin to remember by sight the words that are not underlined. Then you will not need to read them for him. Or the student may try to sound out the words not underlined. Tell him you will give him ways to sound out these words later.

Remember that some children will know just what to do and hardly need to have help. To others the task is surprisingly difficult. I cannot emphasize enough that if your child struggles, do not think he is dull. This process he is learning may create greater demands upon his neurological makeup than it does on that of other children. Be patient!

If you have a child who has difficulty putting these words together when using this procedure, you may say to yourself that this system will never work. It is too cumbersome. You can easily be fooled into thinking that constant drill by exposing the child to flash cards is simpler and faster. Just remember that the sight drill process is faster, and the child may retain the first hundred words fairly easily, but beware! After the initial success, the breakdown takes place. Large numbers of students cannot continuously store words by visual exposure of the overall shape of the word. These children *must* use conscious effort to unlock the phonic elements of the words. Therefore, I earnestly urge you to give the teaching of this decoding (analyzing) procedure your wholehearted effort. It takes time before you meet with the successful results of the automatic reading of words. In the long run, however, you will be duly rewarded. Your child will be building skills he needs throughout his school years.

Using the Typewriter

If you have a typewriter, the child can type some of the words he is learning to read. This adds one more technique to anchor words in the mind.

Cut a piece from a discarded postcard to fit down the center of the letters on the typewriter, between *T Y*, *G H*, and *B N*. Tell your child his left fingers stay on the left side and his right fingers on the right side. This reinforces right and left procedures. It also prepares the child for using all his fingers in typing at a later date when he has full coordination. At this time, he will probably only have full strength in his index fingers. However, I have occasionally had very young children who could manage the correct fingers for touch-typing.

Pick out a few words in each lesson for his typing. When teaching the long *o* with silent *a* in the word *toad*, have the pupil type *oa*, space, *oa*, space, for an entire line. Then have the child type several times the letter *t* with spaces between the letters. After this he can type *toa*, space, *toa*, space, several times followed by typing the single letter *d*, space, *d*, space. Then he is ready to type the whole word *toad* for a full row. Before he starts typing the whole word *toad*, ask your student to spell the word *toad* orally. Now he can type the word. After he has finished typing a row of the word *toad*, ask him to read the word he has typed. Do not be surprised if he has difficulty reading this word he has just tackled. Remember he is concentrating on new skills. If the child has trouble with this typing exercise, you will be observing one more example of the complexities of the learning process. His troubles are the normal growth struggles, which can be just as awkward as maneuvering that new bicycle.

To Buy or Not to Buy! If you feel affluent and want to buy a typewriter, do not buy a child's typewriter. The letters are not arranged in professional order and the instrument is not sturdy enough for serious typing. It is better to buy an old, workable, secondhand model than to buy a toy or a minimal portable machine. (Watch the sales for a good portable.)

I would insist that the child be allowed to type only his lessons (no fooling around with the margin buttons unless you feel confident of his mechanical ability). He should be told that this machine is normally for adults only, because the parts are sensitive and can be easily broken. You are giving your child a special privilege that will be withdrawn if he does not obey your rules. Your other children should have to obey the same rules you set up for the use of the typewriter. *Never* let them move the typewriter. Even with the most careful child, I have seen too many typewriters dropped and, of course, broken.

SILLY SENTENCES

1. Is the <u>coat</u> on the <u>toad</u>?
2. Is the <u>toad</u> on the <u>goat</u>?
3. The <u>coat</u> is on the <u>goat</u>.
4. The <u>toad</u> is on the <u>coat</u>.
5. The <u>toad</u> is on the <u>coat</u> on the <u>goat</u>.

LESSON 4

Phonics: The letters *l* and *r* and long *o* in *oa* (Review)

Start this lesson by reviewing the sounds of the consonants. Then ask your student to look at the illustrations while you teach the following material.

c as in *coat* (like the opening in the cuff of a coat).

g as in the word *go*

d as in the word *duck*

t as in *tee* (*shirt*)

Your student is going to use two more letters in this lesson, *l* and *r*. The letter *l* will be just like the beginning of *t* without the crossbar. The letter *l* has the sound of the *l* in the word *load*.

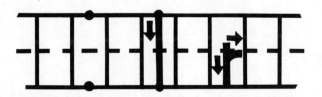

The letter *r* is a stick starting in the middle of the horizontal dotted line tracing down to the solid line. Your pupil then traces back over the line and arches over to greet the space away from that resting hand. Your child can say, "Bye, hand," as he arches out. (Lefty says, "Hi, hand.")

The sound of *r* is like the first sound of the word *road*. (The top piece of the letter *r* is running away from the stick piece. It is running away from the hand that holds the paper.) Keep asking your child what the sounds of these letters are as you print them on cards to hang up around the house.

Have your student look at the Word List. The column at the left has the letter combinations that start each word. If your student has difficulty blending the first letter to the long *o* in the word column, point your pencil to the two-letter combination. Ask your pupil the sound of the vowel, then the sound of the first letter, then the blend of the two letters. Now you can point to the full word. Can he complete it? If your child is having difficulty, you can ask him to look at the word and then you can take a card to blank out the last two letters. Again point to the vowel, ask for its sound loud and long, then the sound of the first letter, followed by the blend.

After your student reads the sentences, have him print these new words on the lined paper you prepare. Dictate a word emphasizing the long *o* sound. Ask him what vowel he hears. Repeat the word with emphasis on the first consonant. Ask what that first letter is. Can he print these letters? If your pupil has trouble remembering the shape of the letter *c*, state that it looks like the sleeve opening of his coat. Be sure he begins his letter formation on the starting point. After your student hears the word *coat* he may print *cot*. Do not be impatient. The beginning student is trying to remember many things you have told him. The pupil who has perceptual problems may spell the word correctly aloud and then proceed to put a garbled form on paper.

If the student has left out the *a* in the word *coat*, ask him what letter sometimes likes to stand beside long *o*. This is *o*'s friend, who looks just like *o* but leans on a stick. It is the letter **a**.

Find something your student does well and praise him. Keep praising often.

NOTE: When you give the consonant sound, try not to add a vowel to it. Your student may be saying *cä*, which is *c* with an extra vowel. He cannot smoothly add the long vowel because it will come out *cäo*.

I have had students who would sound the word out *cäoat* but then quickly make the correction. The adult beginning reader can make this adjustment. It is better to have the schoolchild drop the extra vowel sound when trying to add the long vowel to the consonant.

WORD LIST

co	coat
co	coal
go	goat
lo	load
to	toad
ro	roar
ro	road

SILLY SENTENCES

1. The <u>toad</u> is on the <u>load</u> on the <u>road</u>.
2. A <u>load</u> of <u>coal</u> is on the <u>road</u>.
3. The <u>goat</u> can <u>roar</u>.
4. Can the <u>toad</u> <u>roar</u>?
5. The <u>coal</u> is in the <u>load</u> on the <u>road</u>.

LESSON 5

Phonics: The long *o* in the *oa* pattern

The following list of sentences is for the student who needs practice with the words that end in *d* and *t*. You read the words that are not underlined (unless he can). The student decodes the underlined words with the Seven Special Steps. If the pupil decodes the word incorrectly, do not repeat it for him. Keep pointing your pencil (not your finger) to the *o*. Ask what sound it makes. Have him speak aloud the *o* and drag the sound out, then proceed with the rest of the steps.

WORD LIST

coat   goat   road   toad   load

SILLY SENTENCES

1. The goat has a coat.
2. The coat is on the goat.
3. I have a coat.
4. I have a goat.
5. Is the coat on the goat?
6. Is the toad on the goat?
7. The goat is on the coat.
8. The toad is on the coat.
9. The toad is on the coat on the goat.
10. Is the coat on the toad and the goat?

LESSON 6

Phonics: The letter *m*

The letter *m* gives children trouble right through to the upper grades, if it is not well anchored at this time. The dyslexic child has a great struggle deciding whether he has made *m* or *n*. Some children also see *m* as the letter *w*. I leave the letters *w* and *n* for later lessons, when the letter *m* is well established. Notice that I have the student print the letter *m* almost like the written letter. This eliminates later confusion when your student changes from printing to writing. There are three humps. Have your pupil count aloud one hump, two humps, three humps. Put the dot in the left bottom corner. Your pupil is to shoot his pencil up to the dotted line, arch out and very quickly go down, counting one hump, retrace that last line, arch out and quickly come down to the bottom line, counting two humps. Now up again, arch out and down, counting three humps. Spend this lesson making *m*'s and spelling the words *foam* and *roam*. If your child has no trouble with these letters, go on to the next lesson.

M has the sound of the beginning *m* in the word *more*.

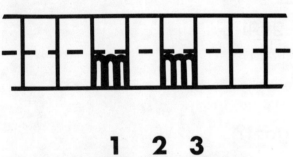

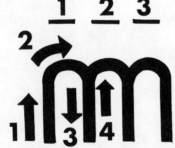

LESSON 7

Extra Phonics: The letter *m* and the long *o* in the *oa* (continued)

Some students have trouble catching the sound difference between *m* and *n*, especially at the end of a word. Remind this student that for the letter *m* he hangs on to the sound longer than he does *n*. The letter *m* has more humps, too. Drag out the sound of mmmmmmmmmmmmmm (not its alphabet name but that sound as in *more*).

WORD LIST

foam   roam   moan   Joan

SILLY SENTENCES

1. I can load coal on the road.
2. The goat can loaf on the road.
3. The coat is on the toad.
4. I can load the coat on the goat.
5. The goat can roar.
6. A load of coal is on the road.
7. The goat can roam on the road.
8. The foam is on the toad.
9. Can the toad roam on the foam?
10. The goat can moan. Can Joan moan?

LESSON 8

Phonics: The letters s, f, and p

The letter *s* starts just like the letter *c,* but instead of pulling down to the bottom line, it swings in to form a *c* in the middle of the square. Then it swings down, shoots across the floor line, and pokes up a bit to say, "Hi, hand." The letter *s* at this time has a hissing sound like the *s* in the word *see.*

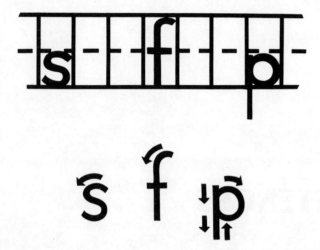

The letter *f* starts like a *c* in the upper part of the box but comes down the middle like the letter *l.* This letter *f* has a cross line in the middle. The sound of *f* is like the beginning sound of the word *feed.*

The letter *p* starts like the letter *r* but continues to make a straight tail. The pencil retraces this line and arches out just like *r* only it circles around, down, and across the bottom line. The shape of the letter *p* should be given much attention, always associating it with a successful *r.* This letter often is confusing to the beginning student. You will notice that *r* and *p* are the first letters in this text to direct themselves to the right. If your child has reversed *p* in the past, be sure to explain how *p* starts. Remember g has a *tail* but it is an *o*-starting letter. *P* has a tail but it is a *stick*-starting letter like *r.* The letter *p* has the sound of the first letter in the word *pet.*

You can spend this entire lesson just reviewing the printing of letters if your child needs correction of past bad habits. This is a good time for more spelling review, too. If, however, your child is ready, you can go to the next lesson.

LESSON 9

Phonics: The letters *j* and *i* and long *o* in *oa* (continued)

Tell your student that the letter *j* is just like the letter **g** without the *o* part. A little dot spouts out of the top. The sound is like the *j* in the word *jump*. Sometimes all of these letters your student is learning change into special shapes. We call these capital letters. These letters are just topped off with some straight extra lines. The names of people start with capital letters, and the first word in each of these sentences you have been reading starts with a capital letter. Capital *J* starts like *I* then turns into a tail on the bottom line and puts a straight line on top. The capital letter *I* starts like the letter *l* and puts a line across the top and the bottom.

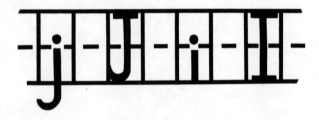

You will have to explain that *Joad* in the sentences below is an old-fashioned boy's name.

SILLY SENTENCES

1. I have a coat.
2. Joad has a coat.
3. The goat has a coat.
4. The toad can roam on the road.
5. The soap has foam.
6. Can the toad roam on the foam?
7. Joad has foam on the coat.
8. Joad can roam on the road.
9. Joad has a load of coal.
10. The load of coal is on the road.

LESSON 10

Phonics: Long *a* in *ai* and letters *i, h, b, n*

Tell your student that letter *a* has to be quiet when *o* stands first in line. Now *a* can leave and become the first vowel. *A* can say his name if he can find a friend to stand beside him. Because *a* leans on a stick he decides to choose a stick friend, the letter *i*. This letter *i* wants to stay right beside the stick on *a*. The letter *i* spouts a dot out of his stick. The combination is *ai*.

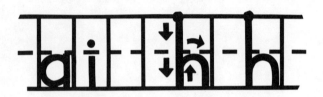

Explain to your student that the letter *i* is silent when it sits beside *a*. Tell the child to remember that in those peanut butter and jelly words, the first vowel makes the sound. It says its name. Second vowel is silent. Explain to your student that when he sees two vowels together, he must make his mind shut out any sound for the second vowel.

The next letter he is to study is the letter *h*. This letter starts as a straight line. Then when the pencil hits the bottom line, push it back up this stick half-way. Now arch out like he does for the letter *r*. Then pull that arch down to the floor of the solid line.

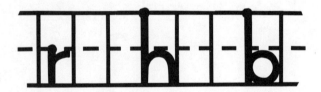

The letter *h* has the sound of the *h* as in huff. He must have to huff and puff to make the sound.

The letter *b* is just like *h* only he tucks a bottom on the letter. The sound of the letter *b* can give some students trouble. In school the student may have learned the sound is like the *b* in the word *bus*. He then anchors the short-vowel sound of *u* to the *b*. Then when he tries to say the word *bait*, he struggles with *buait*. Ask your pupil to make the *b*

sound just bubble out of his mouth and try not to add any vowel sound to it. This trouble in adding a vowel to the consonant when you teach the consonant sound can create problems. Try to keep the consonant sound pure.

The letter *n* is made like the letter *r* but it arches right down to the floor line. The letter *n* has the sound of *n* in *no*. This gives your student two of the short words, *go* and *no*.

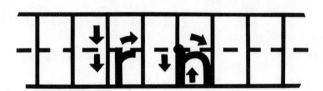

LESSON 11

Phonics: Long *a* in *ai* (continued)

Have the child look at the word and count the vowels. Tell him to cross out the second vowel in his mind. He is to repeat the first vowel aloud. Now take the 1″ × 2″ card and block off the last two letters of the word. Have the child blend the first consonant to the vowel. If he gets the vowel sound wrong, point your pencil to the first vowel, *a*. Ask what the sound of that letter is. Ask him to speak that vowel loud and long. Point to the left column. Can he blend the two letters together? When he does this, have your pupil repeat the consonant and vowel combination. Now take the card off the word and have your student blend in the last consonant.

This process is extremely difficult for some children. Be very patient. When the child does not succeed, do not show irritation. This procedure stimulates the brain to perceive the letter symbol, then to signal to the auditory receptor area, which must vocalize the sounds. Then the brain can process the word. These pathways in some brains are sluggish. This exercise strengthens the brain passages needed for successful reading.

WORD LIST

ma	mail	sa	sail
na	nail	ra	rain
pa	pail	ha	hair

SILLY SENTENCES

1. Joan can roam on the road.
2. The mail can be in the load on the road.
3. The nail can be in the load.
4. The nail is in the load of coal.
5. I have a nail in the pail.
6. The rain is in the pail.
7. Joad has a nail in the pail.
8. The goat has a tail.
9. The rain is in the hair of the goat.
10. The goat can moan and roar.
11. Joan has rain on her coat.
12. Joan can go for a sail.
13. I can sail in the boat.
14. The goat can go for a sail in the boat.
15. Can Joad sail in the boat?
16. No, Joad can not sail in the boat.

PARENTS: There are some words in these sentences the child is not ready to analyze. Read them for him. These are the words to be read and are called Feed Words: on, the, be, in, is, has, of, and, for, not, can.

61

LESSON 12

Phonics: Review

Ask your student to name letters he now knows. Have him print the letters o a c g d t l f s i j r n p h b l J

Can he tell you which of these letters are vowels? Do not be surprised if he cannot recall these vowels. Tell him that big round *o* is a vowel and that letter a that starts like *o* but leans on the stick to make the letter *a* is a vowel. Also, remind your pupil that *o* likes his silent friend *a* beside him. (If you have a typewriter, have your child type *oa*, space, *oa*, space, several times. Ask him what the big name is for these letters. Answer: vowels.)

When *a* is the first vowel, what other vowel does *a* like beside him? The letter *a* likes that stick letter *i* beside him. (This vowel pattern can be typed. Follow the instructions on typing in Lesson 3.)

On lined paper, rule red dotted lines just above the center of the spaces. Now have your student print the new words he knows. Sound out one of the words. See if he can spell it aloud and then print the word.

Spelling list: coat, goat, coal, load, toad, road, roar, foam, roam.

If this is very difficult for your student, have him print only two or three words. Then you can stop the lesson for the day. If this is very easy for your child, go to the next lesson.

LESSON 13

Phonics: Review

Have your student reread the sentences in the previous lessons that have the *ai* pattern. If he makes a mistake, do not say the word for him. Make him decode the word with the Seven Special Steps.

Spelling list: mail, nail, pail, sail, rain, hair.

See if your student can print these *ai* words. (Prepare the lined paper with the dots.) Do be very patient. Spelling dictated words is extremely difficult for many students. Repeat the word *mail*. Ask your pupil what vowel he hears. If he cannot tell you, hold up separate cards with the vowels he has now been exposed to (*o a i*). Repeat the word *mail*. Ask him to point to the vowel on the card he thinks is correct. After he realizes the vowel is *a*, ask him what silent friend stands beside *a*. (Answer: stick friend *i* likes to be next to *a*.) Repeat the word *mail* again. Ask your student what letter he hears as the first letter in the word. Have him print *m*. Now he can print the vowel he heard, then the silent vowel friend (*a i*).

Repeat the word *mail* again! Emphasize the letter *l*. Your student can now print *l*. Try *nail*, *pail*, and *sail*. If he does well, add *rain* and *hair*.

Be sure to praise your child for trying even though he may have had minimal success. Tell him you are pleased he is working so hard.

Your student can now decode seventeen words. In later review lessons, he will add more vowel digraphs, which will add up to a reading vocabulary of 158 words. There are 205 layer-cake words (words with consonant–long vowel–consonant–silent *e*), which he will also learn to decode. In a very short time your child will be able to decode 363 words. It would take him almost a year of classwork to learn that number of words by sight; that is, if he were able to learn by the look-and-say method (which many students cannot do).

By the strict rules of phonics, the words *roar*, *pair*, and *hair* should not be included in this list because the letter *r* changes the word into what seems almost to be two syllables — *ro ar* and *ha er* or *pa er*. Most students manage the sound. If you run into difficulty, do not make the pupil decode the *r* part of the word. Give the last part to him. He soon makes the adjustment.

WORD LIST

co	coat	coal		ma	mail
go	goat			na	nail
to	toad			pa	pail
lo	load	loan		sa	sail
ro	roar	roam		ra	rain
fo	foam			ha	hair
so	soap				
Jo	Joad				
mo	moan				

LESSON 14

Phonics: Patterns

Ask your student to look at the words on the *oa-ai* word list page. Point your pencil (not your finger, it is too large) to the *oa* in several words. Tell your child you want him to think of the *o* as crunchy peanut butter. This first vowel, *o,* makes the sound. The *a* is the jelly in the sandwich. The letters on each side of *oa* are the bread. Now you have peanut butter and jelly sandwich words. (Refer to Lesson 29 for the sandwich concept.)

Your child may not understand what you mean immediately, not because the concept is difficult but for another reason. Ask your pupil to underline with his pencil the peanut butter and jelly part of the word. If your child succeeds, continue with the *ai* words. If he does *not* succeed, you will need to read the next paragraph.

Suppose your student did not really listen to you even though he seemed to be attentive. (If he has met failure in school, he has fallen into the not-hearing habit.) Reminding the child in an irritated voice that he is not listening will not correct the bad habit. Instead, say to him in a joking way, "I bet you did not hear me when I was just talking to you. Sometimes I do not pay attention when someone speaks to me. This time listen carefully and stop me when you do not understand what I am saying. Then I can start over again." Your child may be so astounded that nobody made him feel guilty, he still will not know how to listen! Your loving concern will eventually cure the problem.

WORD LIST

ba	bail	bait	
fa	fail		
ja	jail		
ha	hail	hair	
ma	main	maid	mail
na	nail		
pa	pail	pair	
ra	rain	rail	raid
sa	sail		
ta	tail		
wa	wait		

LESSON 15

Phonics: Letters *u* and *w*

Explain to your student that he will learn two new letters: *u* and *w*. To make the letter *u* he starts in the corner where he sees the red dot. He pulls his pencil down straight then curves around like the bottom of the letter *o*. Then he pushes his pencil up the other side of the box. The letter *u* leans on a stick just like the letter *a* does. Your student will work with the sounds of *u* later.

Printing the letter *w* is just like hitching two *u*'s together. That is why it is called *double* u. The sound of *w* is not anything like its alphabet name. It sounds more like the alphabet name of *y*!

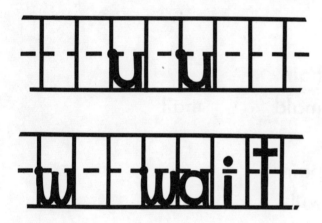

Print a card with the word *wait*. Follow the Seven Special Steps. Have your student practice several *u*'s and several *w*'s. If you want to review previous work, you can do this to complete the lesson. You can start the *would* and *could* section tomorrow.

LESSON 16

Extra Words

Print *ould* four times on a piece of paper. Show the student how to trace with pencil around the letters of *ould*. Use the same sequence as is numbered in the illustration. The pupil starts at the number 1 corner, goes to 2, then to 3, etc. If the student goes ahead too eagerly and traces inaccurately, do not correct him with an impatient voice. Just state, "Let's try that again this way." If he gets upset with his inadequacy, you should do the tracing for him while he watches. This type of close tracing is really too fine for some students. However, the process of visualizing the shape is important. Tell the student it was very hard for you when you were his age. He will not appreciate your saying, "That is wrong, I told you how to do it, but you did not listen." You may think he is not listening, but if he is failing, the scolding will *not* help him listen.

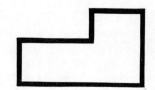 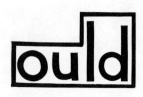

On a lined piece of paper, print *ould* three times (in black ink), quite far apart. Tell him what sound this is. Ask him to repeat the sound several times. Now show the student that you can put *c,* or *w* (in red ink), in front of these letters. Repeat the words for him. Have him repeat the words.

Draw this traced pattern without the letters. Ask the child what picture he wants to make out of this shape.

The words will be used so often they will eventually become automatic. Tell your pupil there are some words he is not to try to sound out. You will help him try to remember by special clues.

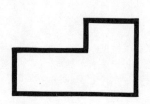 

Explain to your pupil that this is the shape that *ould* fits into. Draw this pattern again in four places within the space of lined paper. Print *ould* into one of the boxes. Ask your pupil to print *ou* in the right spot in one of the boxes. Then have him print the *ld*. Repeat in the other boxes.

LESSON 17

Phonics: Long *e* in *ee*

Now your student meets a new vowel, the letter *e*. Have him draw a line through the middle of the several lower boxes. See below.

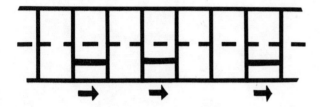

Now tell your pupil to make the letter *c* after he has drawn the line across the box.

This vowel *e* often likes his twin brother to stand beside him. Two *e*'s are the filling between the letters that act like bread. Print the following words on cards: *deer, feet, feel, feed, heel, need, peep, seed, seem*. Tell your child to look at these words. Can he point with his pencil to *e* with his twin brother *e*? The *e* will be the middle sound in the word. Can he print the word *deer*? Ask what vowel sound he hears (you will have to emphasize the *e* sound in the word). Have him print that first letter he hears, then the vowel *e*, then the twin brother *e*. What is the final sound he hears? (Emphasize the *r* sound.) Now can your student read the words on the cards? (Use the Seven Special Steps.) Your student can now read the Silly Sentences that follow.

The letter *r* in the word *deer* makes the word seem like two syllables. If the child has trouble with the *r* sound, do not make him labor over the word; say it for him.

WORD LIST

be	beef	beet	
de	deer		
fe	feet	feel	feed
ke	keep		
he	heel		
ne	need		
me	meet		
pe	peep	peel	
se	seed	seem	seek
we	week	weed	weep

SILLY SENTENCES

1. Joad <u>sees</u> the <u>deer</u> on the road.
2. Joad could <u>feed</u> the <u>deer</u>.
3. The <u>deer</u> could <u>see</u> the <u>seed</u> in the pail.
4. Would the <u>deer</u> <u>need</u> a coat?
5. Could the <u>deer</u> <u>feel</u> the rain?
6. Joad could <u>meet</u> the <u>deer</u> on the road.
7. Would the <u>deer</u> <u>need</u> the soap?
8. Would the <u>deer</u> <u>feel</u> the soap foam?
9. The <u>deer</u> could <u>meet</u> the toad on the road.
10. Joad would <u>need</u> the pail to <u>feed</u> the <u>deer</u>.

LESSON 18

Phonics: Long *e* in *ea*

In this lesson your student meets long *e* that uses *a* for his friend instead of his twin brother. Before you explain this to your student, ask him if he remembers what friend the letter *a* likes to have beside him. Do not be upset if your child has difficulty recalling. (This will point out the need for review.) Print the letter a while you are asking what letter friend stands next to a. Trace your pencil over the straight line in a. Ask your pupil if this gives him a hint about what letter friend stands beside a. If he cannot remember, calmly explain that the same kind of stick friend that the letter a leans on likes to stand beside a. This letter *i* has a dot on top.

Now ask your student what letter friend *o* likes beside him. Does tracing the *o* give him a hint? *O* likes his friend that is so much like him (round *o*) that leans on a stick (the letter a).

Tell your pupil that in the last lesson he learned about the letter *e* with his twin brother. The letter *e* has another friend. The letter *a* often stands beside *e*. Repeat aloud the combination *ea, ea, ea,* several times. Have your student repeat *ea, ea, ea.* It has a nice slurry sound.

Your student should print *ea* several times. During this lesson have your child print some of the words from the Word List. (Always use the lined paper. Put dotted lines in the spaces.)

LESSON 19

Phonics: Long *e* in *ea* (continued)

NOTE: The vowel digraphs *ea, ei,* and *ie* may be the most confusing combinations in our language because they each have three or more different sounds. Examples: mean, great, bread, and earn. In the Integral Phonics Reading Program the long *e* combination is the only one used during the introductory level. After the student has learned to decode on an automatic basis, using the Seven Special Steps, the irregularities of the English language can be introduced. Strangely enough, the student has very little difficulty with these irregularities if his decoding skills have become strong.

Several words on these vowel digraph lists have two meanings. The words *leap, deal, roar, sail,* etc., can be used as nouns or verbs. Also, there are several homonyms: *heel–heal; seam–seem; weak–week,* etc.

Here some students will realize we can use these words in different ways. If your child stumbles onto this situation, you will need to explain to him that the English language plays some funny tricks. Later he will be given a number of words that can be used in more than one way.

NOTE: Explain to your student that some of these peanut butter and jelly words leave part of the sandwich off. (Refer to Lesson 29 for more detail on the sandwich concept.) Print the words *see* and *bee*. Ask your pupil to point to the first vowel. What is the sound? Now have him repeat the sound of the first letter, then join it onto the vowel sound. The words *air, eat, ear* leave off the first slice of bread.

WORD LIST

be	bead	bean	beat
de	deal	dear	
fe	fear		
ge	gear		
he	heat	hear	
Je	Jean		
le	leaf	lead	leak	leap	lean
me	meal	mean	
ne	near	neat	
pe	peas	peal	peak
re	read	rear	real
se	seal	seam	
te	team		
we	weak		

SILLY SENTENCES

1. Jean could hear the seal leap in the rain.
2. The seal would need to leap in the heat.
3. Jean could see a leaf on the road.
4. The toad could leap.
5. Could the seal leap?
6. Could the seal leap near the toad?
7. Would the toad feel the seal near him?
8. Would the toad feel a fear if the seal would leap near?
9. The seal could hear a leaf as it would sail near.
10. Jean would feel weak if the seal would leap on her.

Feed Words: if, as, it, on, her.

LESSON 20

Extra Words

Review the following words; you should print these words on cards to have in an Extra Word envelope: *could, would, the, a, go, no.* You can print each word on a separate piece of paper and tape it onto the refrigerator, the bathtub, or some unexpected place. These Extra Words will be given gradually throughout the book. The total number of sight words needed by the time the student finishes this book will not exceed ten.

Read the instructions for The Game. Make up a set of cards from the *oa* and *ai* Word Lists before you start this lesson. Tell your student you have a game to play after he reads the Silly Sentences for this lesson.

NOTE: Be sure you are giving rewards and heaps of praise.

The Game

Print each one of the *oa* and *ai* words on individual 1″ × 2″ cards. On nine of the cards, put a colored star or a cross in the middle, below the word. Shuffle all the cards. Place the pack between you and the student. He turns one up and reads it (using the Seven Special Steps). If he reads correctly, he keeps the card. Then it is your turn. You read the card if it does not have a star on it. If there is a star, your pupil gets a chance to read it. He keeps it when he reads it correctly. If he draws a star and reads the word correctly, he can keep the card *and* take any cards you have accumulated; otherwise you get the card *and* his pile!

Keep reminding your student to point his pencil to the first vowel. What is the vowel sound? Then your student sounds the first letter and blends it with the vowel, etc. After your pupil repeats the vowel, you may need to cover up all but the first two letters while he sounds the word out.

Show real enthusiasm while you are playing the game. Express your disgust when you lose your cards. When your child gets the star card, say, "Now maybe I can win the cards back." He will get quite excited trying to beat you.

(You can make a new stack of cards for the new words as your child progresses.)

LESSON 21

Phonics: Review

Most students need from three to five days repeat of each of the previous lessons. If you have been going too fast, it is time for review. The following pages have Silly Sentences for *oa, ai, ee,* and *ea* patterns. If your student seems to have grasped the concepts, you can skip these sentences even though he is still at the decoding level. As he reads each group of sentences, let him put a sticker beside them or he can draw a design.

SILLY SENTENCES

1. The toad can roam in the rain.
2. The toad can sail on the soap.
3. The goat can sail in the rain.
4. Joan can soak in a pail.
5. Gail can go on the road.

1. The mail is in a pail.
2. We can sail in the rain.
3. The boat has a main sail.
4. Gail could load the pail.
5. Gail could sail in the boat.

1. I have a deer. I feed the deer.
2. The goat can meet the toad on the road.
3. I could keep the nail.
4. Joad can keep the toad.
5. Keep the foam on the soap.

1. He could heat the bean in the pail.
2. She has meat in the load.
3. The seal and the toad could be in the road.
4. The team could be near.
5. Could the team feel weak?

LESSON 22

Phonics: Letter direction practice

Use the Word List for a spelling and writing lesson. These words require specific directional practice: *rear, near, hear, bean, beat, heat, neat, rail, nail, hail, bail, pail, pair, hair, rain, roar.* (Dictate these words in the sequence given.)

he must print, what the letter looks like, at what point he starts with his pencil, right to left, or left to right, or up to down, or bottom to top — all this in a short period of time, which is a tremendous load on the nervous system.

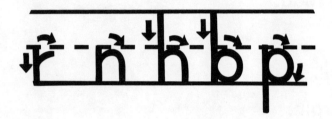

This exercise helps prevent letter reversal. You should use this lesson two or three days in a row. At intervals return to the lesson and repeat it. Do not have the student print this list in columns. Have him print each word consecutively across the paper. This is practice for future sentence work.

rear near

hear bean

You no longer need to make boxes for each letter. After the child prints a word, draw vertical lines, which will represent the space needed between each word. Show him where to start the next word. Some children have no trouble with spacing, others take a long time before they develop the coordination necessary for neat printing. You have to remember your student is trying to remember many things while he prints just one letter! He has had to listen to the sound you made, decide what letter

LESSON 23

Phonics: Letter direction practice (continued)

Use this list for another spelling lesson (do not use it on the same days that you use the *r, n, h, b, p,* lesson): *coal, coat, goat, load, toad, deaf, feed, lead.*

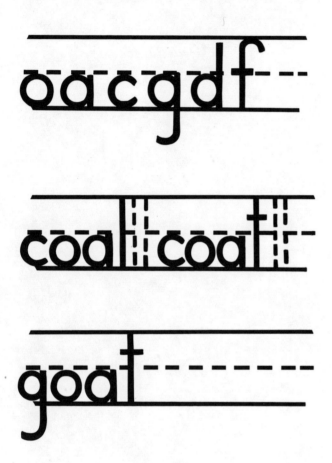

LESSON 24

Phonics: Three new letters: k, v, y

The three consonants *k*, *v*, *y*, give your student the rest of the letters in the alphabet that he needs. *Z*, *q*, *x*, the letters remaining that have not been taught, will be given after your child has had a great deal of practice with the three basic line directions he has been using, which are:

The letter *k* has the same sound as the hard *c* your pupil has been using.

The *k* starts just like the letter *h*. It retraces the line just as he does with *h*. However, when he would curve out, he will instead point out a little way to the right top corner of the box. Then, he should put his pencil at the middle of the tall line and pull it down to the right corner.

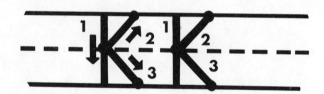

Do not worry whether your student's *k* looks more like the capital *K* than the lower case letter. With practice he will correct this. Have him make several *k*'s. Can he now print the word *keep*? What vowel sound does he hear? This long *e* wants his twin brother beside him. The word starts with this new letter *k*. Continue with the twin brother; then what is the last letter?

Before you teach the letter *v*, put two red dots in the upper corners of the lower box and a red dot in the middle of the bottom line of the box. Now ask your student to start where he starts with the letter *r*. Point down to the bottom dot, then up to the right-side dot. The dyslexic student often confuses the sound of *v* with the sound of *f*. Demonstrate to him that he can feel the breeze coming

out of his mouth for the letter *f* when he gives it a good strong sound. Also, he should feel the *v* sound in his throat.

Can your child print the word *veal*? Repeat the word *veal*. Ask what vowel sound does he hear? This long *e* sound does not want his twin brother; he wants his friend. Can he remember what friend long *e* likes (silent *a*)?

You will need to explain that beefsteak comes from big cows but veal is a meat that comes from little cows that are not grown up (calves).

If you feel your child has had enough with these two new letters, just review some of the Silly Sentences of previous lessons. Then tomorrow teach him the letter *y*, which begins like the letter *v*. When your student makes the second line for *v*, he just keeps going to form the *y*. The *y* sound is like the beginning of the word *yes*.

LESSON 25

Extra Words

In a special envelope, keep 1″ × 2″ cards for sight words. Print the following words (add the Extra Words of each lesson as you proceed): *a, to, do, the*.

Usually these words are automatically recognized because they are used so often in the text. If the child is not able to sight-read these words, let him use the word *a* as its alphabet name. Just keep reminding him that when *a* stands for a whole word we usually change its sound to *a*. (The dictionary signal for this sound is, usually, too confusing at this point!) Many basic reading programs do not allow the student to pronounce the word *a* like long *a*. The theory behind this decision is that the student will never be able to handle words like *above, away, along*, etc. Any students I have exposed to the Integral Phonics Reading Program sort this out with no trouble.

Now take the word *to*. Tell the student he is going to be able to do many tricks with *o*. He can call it by its alphabet name *o*. We call this a long *o*. There are three little words that end in long *o*: *go, so, no*. (Use the Seven Special Steps to puzzle out these words.) There is another *o* sound in the words *do* and *to*. It is a pulled-out sound, *dooooo-ooooo*. That tall *d* pushes the *o* into that special sound. The tall *t* also pushes that *o*. Have the child make a tall *d*, follow it with a long line of *o*'s. Then he can print a tall *t* with many *o*'s.

You can introduce the *th* sound at this time because the child will soon enjoy *then, there,* and *that*. Tell him to try hard with the *th* sound but not to worry if he has trouble, because most people in Europe (get out your map for your student) who do not have that sound in their language never learn to get their tongues around the sound (and we think they are charming). Your child can take his time and beat the Europeans.*

The word *the* is fairly simple but quite important because this is the first exposure to the *th* sound, which is used in numerous words that will be treated as sight words. In many reading programs, the students are still struggling with the *th* sight words up through the fifth grade. If we anchor these sticklers slowly, we can avoid future troubles. (The *th* has two sounds but the fine difference is not important at this time.)

Review these words, *a, to, do, the*. Spread the cards on the table, ask your child to find *to* and *do*. Sound out the *t* and the *o*, reminding him these are the tall letters that push the *o* sound. Have him puzzle out the other words.

* Tell your pupil to keep his tongue in back of his front teeth when saying *th*. If the tongue comes out in front of the teeth, a lisping sound takes place when there is an *s* in the *th* word.

LESSON 26

Phonics: Long *a* (layer-cake pattern)

Up to this point your child has been dealing with the sandwich patterned words. The two vowels in between the consonants are the crunchy peanut butter and jelly between the slices of bread. Now your child is going to look at long vowel words, which are layer-cake words. Tell your student to look at the Word List in this lesson. Each one of these words starts with a consonant; the consonant is the cake. Next comes the vowel frosting, then the layer of cake (consonant) ending with *e* frosting. Can he find any word on this page that does not end in the vowel *e*? Each one of these layer-cake words has a long *a* in it. Turn to the next page; ask your student if he can tell whether these words are peanut butter and jelly words or layer-cake words. He may not be able to register the fact that these two pages of words look different from the long-vowel words he has been reading. Have you been making cards for each word your student has been learning? Now print these new words on 1″ × 2″ cards. Place the peanut butter and jelly words on one side of the table; spread the layer-cake words on the other side of the table. Underline the two vowels in a few of the sandwich words — n<u>ai</u>l t<u>ai</u>l n<u>ea</u>t h<u>ea</u>t. Count first vowel, second vowel. Ask which vowel says its name. If your pupil hesitates, explain that first vowel has all the fun. He can shout his name. Second vowel has to keep his name to himself. (Your student later has to learn that the vowel in the word *cap* does not say its alphabet name, it says short *a*.)

Now underline the *a* and the *e* on a few of the other cards — c<u>a</u>k<u>e</u>, m<u>a</u>k<u>e</u>, b<u>a</u>k<u>e</u>. Tell your student *a* is first vowel, *e* is second vowel. Once again first vowel has all the fun. He can shout his name. Poor *e* (the second vowel) has to be quiet.

You are ready to use the Seven Special Steps to have your child read these words. If he has trouble blending the first letter to the vowel, use the exercise column. Now your student can read the Silly Sentences with long *a*.

Starting with this lesson your student will be reading a little story each time. The vocabulary is still limited, so the stories are awkward. That is why I call them Silly Stories. If your child comments on the limitations of the stories, you can explain that they will make more sense as he acquires more words. Have your student review the Word List.

Then have him read the new story always using the Seven Special Steps.

WORD LIST

ba	bake	base				
ca	cake	cape	came	cage	case	care
da	date	dare	dame	Dave		
fa	face	fame	fake	fate	fade	
ga	gate	game	gave			
ha	hate					
ja	Jake	Jane				
la	lake	lame	lane	late	lace	
ma	make	mate	mane	made		
na	name					
pa	pale	pave	page	pane		
ra	rate	rake	rave	rare	race	
sa	sage	safe	sale	same	save	
ta	take	tape				
va	vane	vase				
wa	wage	wave				

→

SILLY SENTENCES

1. Jane made a cake.

2. Jake could bake a cake.

3. Jake would hate to make a cake.

4. Jane gave the cake to Jake.

5. Jake could save the cake for the cake sale.

6. Would Jane bake a cake for the goat?

7. The goat would take the cake.

8. Jake could save the cake he made.

9. Jake gave the game to Jane.

10. Jane could race Jake.

SILLY STORY

Jake and the Mean Goat

Dave had a mean goat. Dave gave the goat the name Mate. Jake would meet Dave at the lake. Jake could take Dave for a sail in the boat.

The mean goat would moan and roar if Jake would leap on the boat. Mate, the mean goat, would seem to be in a rage if Jake made a leap to the boat.

Jake gave up. He would not go on the boat.

Feed Words: had, not, on, up, for, if, in.

LESSON 27

Extra Words

Review the words in the envelope: *could, would, the, a, no, go, to, do.*

Phonics: Capital letters

Reread the previous story as review. The following lesson in printing will involve capital letters. Explain the fact that sometimes letters change their shape from small letters to big ones called capitals.

On lined paper with the red dotted lines, show your student how the capital *C* is just like the small *c* but it uses up the whole box. (Have your pupil practice both capital and small letters.)

The capital letter *S* is just like the small letter *s*. Your pupil will make a *c* in the top box, then swing around in the bottom box.

Tell your child that the capital letter *W* in printed form in books is more pointed than what he makes. Capital *W* uses the whole box. The letter is really just like small *w* but the sides are taller.

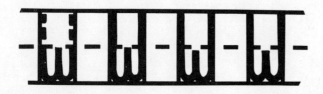

After you finish the work with capitals, have your student review the long *a* Word List and reread the sentences. If your child still is struggling with the blending of each word, have him work on each lesson three to five days in a row. Then go to the next phonic integral.

LESSON 28

Extra Words

Add the words *they, and.* The word *and* is used so often the child eventually remembers it by sight.

Print the word *they* on one of the 1″ × 2″ cards. Block off the last letter *y* (with a card; remember, your finger is too thick). Ask your student if he remembers this word *the.* Repeat the word *the* and blur on a long *a* sound. Help the student this way each time you review the word. Your child will be learning the spelling of: the, they, there, their. Each of these words begins with the word *the.* Teaching this sequence avoids the misspelling of *they* as *thay* and *their* as *thier.*

Phonics: Long *i* (layer-cake pattern)

Have your student work with the Word List for long *i.* Then have your pupil read the story on the next day.

There are several points you will need to explain. The word *leave* is in this story. Your child can decode the word *leave.* Here we have three vowels. Some children are quick to point this out, others just see the *ea* pattern and ignore the last *e.* If your child notices this, explain to him that sometimes our language gets mixed up. He will meet a few words that do this: *heave, breeze, tease, lease, peeve.* These words really have *e* frosting on the peanut butter and jelly form.

Point out to your student that when *y* is at the end of a word, it may do all kinds of strange things. After *a,* the letter *y* hides its sound. It is silent (*bay, day, gay,* etc.).

After the letters *b* and *m,* the letter *y* takes the sound of long *i.* Examples: *my, by.*

You will need to tell your student that the letter *c* has two sounds. He has been using the hard sound of *c* (like *k*) as in *cake.* Now he will meet *ce;* the *c* takes the sound like *s.*

WORD LIST

bi	bike	bite	
di	dime	dike	dine	dice
fi	fire	fine	five	file
hi	hide	hike	hive	
ki	kite			
li	lime	line	life	lice
mi	mile	mine	Mike	mice
ni	nice			
pi	pile	pipe	pine	
ri	ride	rice		
si	side	size		
ti	tide	tile	time	tire
wi	wife	wine	wire	wide
vi	vine			

SILLY STORY

Could Mike Ride His Bike?

Mike would like to ride a mile on his bike. Mike would not dare leave his goat. So Mike could not ride a mile on his bike. The tame goat would not be fine if Mike would leave on his bike.

The tame goat would roam and hike on the wide road. The tame goat would not like to be alone. If Mike would ride his bike, the tame goat would hide on Mike. He would bite Jane and Joan if they came to see Mike.

You could see that Mike could not ride a mile on his bike.

Feed Words: on, his, not, if, and, so, alone, that.

LESSON 29

Extra Words

Review *could, would, a, to, do, and, the, they*. Your student has been exposed to the word *go* used as a verb. That word *go* is just like the front part of the word *goat*. The word *no* rhymes with *go*. Now you can review the word *so*. (These words are little, tiny long-vowel words that fit in with the phonics lessons.)

Phonics: Long *o* (layer-cake pattern) and three new words

Your child can read the Word List for long *o*. Remind him that this list is the layer-cake list (long *o* with silent *e* frosting). You may want to say that when you look at these layers, you are looking at the layer cake from the side. I take four blocks of wood and paste the letters on them so that when you turn the "cake" on its side the child sees the word. You might think that all this maneuvering would be confusing to the child. Instead, he is fascinated with the puzzle of the layer cake with *e* frosting. (Teachers have told me that the use of this concept has given them their first success in teaching these long-vowel, silent *e* words. Most students just do not understand the traditional explanation of the structure of these words.)

There are three tiny long-vowel words your student can manage now. You can tell your child that there are a few words in our language that have ended up with only two letters. He already knows *go, no, so* (point to the *o*, then to the first letter). Now he can learn three new words, *he, be, we*. Do not give the word *me* yet. The letter **m** is the reverse of **w** and may confuse him. Let the child use the word *we* many times before you add *me*.

Give a spelling lesson of: *go, no, so, he, be, we.*

The *se* in the underlined words in the Word List has a *z* sound. The student uses these words in conversation; thus, he has little difficulty correcting the sound. You can call attention to the fact that the hissing sound of the letter *s* changes to a harder hissing sound in some words.

Peanut Butter and Jelly Words

Layer-Cake Words

WORD LIST

bo	bone	bore			
co	cone	core	cove	code	coke
do	dome				
go	go				
ho	hole	home	hope	ho<u>se</u>	
jo	joke				
lo	lone				
mo	more	mole			
no	note	no<u>se</u>			
po	pole	poke			
to	tone				
ro	rope	ro<u>se</u>			
so	sore				

→

SILLY STORY

Hope, the Goat

Joan has a tame goat like the goat Mike has. Joan's goat would not be mean. Joan gave a name to the tame goat. The goat has the name of Hope.

Joan could not make the tame goat do things. Joan had a hope that the name of Hope could make the goat go and do things.

Joan would poke the goat in the nose. A poke with a pole would not be nice. A poke with a pole could make a sore.

Joan gave up hope. The goat would not be mean, but the goat with the name of Hope would not do things for Joan. Joan has no hope for Hope, the goat.

Feed Words: has, had, things, of, not, that, with, in, but, for.

LESSON 30

Extra Words

Review *could, would, a, to, do, and, the, they.* Add *at, that* to the envelope of Extra Words. Each of these words has only one vowel. This vowel does not have the alphabet name for its sound. Sound out the *a* in a distasteful manner like the sound you make when you do not like something. Show your student how he can put *th* in front of *at* and get the word *that.*

Phonics: Long u (layer-cake pattern)

Use the same directions that you used in previous lessons. Be sure your student is using the Seven Special Steps to decode the words.

The word *ice* is used in the story. Show your child how it is part of the word *nice.*

When you come to the word *became,* block off *came* with a 1″ × 2″ card. Your child reads *be.* Now block off this front part of the word until he decodes *came.* Help him repeat *became.*

Have you been playing The Game with your child? You can keep changing the words as he meets a new list. Do not try to use more than twenty or thirty words for a game; otherwise, the time drags. Just keep varying the words.

Keep praising!

Explain to your student that he will meet words that sound the same but are not spelled the same and do not have the same meanings. For example: *week, weak; meet, meat.*

WORD LIST

cu	cube	cure	cute
fu	fuse		
hu	huge		
mu	mule		
pu	pure		

SILLY STORY

Jake and the Cute Toad

Jake had a huge cute toad. Jake could see that the huge cute toad did feel weak. He did not seem to leap like he did the week Mike gave Jake the cute toad.

Jake could see he would have to find a cure for the cute toad. Would a cube of ice make the huge toad feel nice? Would the cube of ice be a cure for the weak toad?

The cube of pure ice would feel nice to the cute toad. Sure enough, the pure cube of ice be<u>came</u> the cure to make the huge toad feel fine.

Feed Words: had, did, that, not, find, of, for, ice, sure, enough.　　　　　　→

SILLY STORY

The Cute Mice

Dave and Mike have a kite. They would like to use* the kite for the five mice. They would have the cute mice ride on the kite.

Jane would not like to have the cute mice ride on the kite. Would the mice like to ride in a cage on a huge mule?

The cute mice would hate to ride on the huge kite. The huge mule would be safe. The kite would not be safe for the cute mice.

* NOTE: Show your student the word *use* is like *fuse* without the *f*.

LESSON 31

Phonics: Capital N, *sh*, *ay*

Spelling: Explain to your student that he will soon be printing full sentences. Each sentence will have one full idea in the group of words. Show him the sentences in the *Silly Stories* he has read. Point to the capital letter that always starts the first word in the sentence, and the period that ends the sentence. Have your pupil point out capital letters in some of the stories. When your child is looking for something to do during the day, give him a newspaper or magazine. Have him underline capital letters. He can also underline words he can find that he has learned to read.

Add another capital letter to your student's list. N starts with the two straight lines. The pencil goes back to that first red dot (in the upper left corner). Push a line down to the opposite bottom corner.

Dictate the following words (ask for capital letters at the beginning of each word): *He, No, So, Go, We, A, I, Dave, Mike, Joan.*

Up to this point, your student has been reading one-syllable words. There have been no prefixes or suffixes. In future lessons, *s* and *ed* will be added to some words. These letters will be underlined. When your child meets a word ending in *s* or *ed*, have him look at the word, then you are to take a card and cover the *s* or *ed*. Have him read the word, then slip the card off, and you add the last sound.

In this lesson you can introduce the sound of *sh*. Tell your student that the letter *s* by itself has the hissing sound and sometimes a hissing with a buzzing sound (to be introduced later. Example: *wise*). When *s* is joined to *h*, the letters make one sound instead of two separate sounds. When your child wants someone to be quiet, he says *shhh*. The letters *sh* take that sound: *she, sheet, shake, shine, shone.* Print these words on cards.

When your student reads these words, ask him what the vowel sound is *first*, then have him use the *sh* sound and join it to the vowel.

Another phonic integral in this lesson is the *ay* sound. Explain to your student that long *a* has another form besides the peanut butter and jelly pattern and the layer-cake pattern. This other form is *ay*. The *y* acts like a vowel so the words still will have first vowel, second vowel. (Second vowel has to keep quiet.)

WORD LIST

ba	bay	ma	May
da	day	na	nay
ga	gay	pa	pay
ha	hay	ra	ray
ja	jay	sa	say
ka	Kay	wa	way

SILLY STORY

Kay and May

Kay and May like to take a day to be by the lake. They sail a boat on the lake. They like the waves the boat makes as they sail.

Kay would say to May that she would like to sail into a bay near the sea. May would say to Kay that she would fear a sail in the bay. The waves in a bay may be huge. The waves in the lake are not huge.

So Kay and May sail on the safe lake in the day time.

Feed Words: as, by, on, in, not, are.

LESSON 32

Change to book print of *a* and *g*

The printed *a* and *g* in most books is too confusing to be used by beginning students at first. Now that your student is printing and reading he will be able to become acquainted with the *a* and *g* used in adult books.

Show your pupil the comparison list of words. Have him read the words. Do not encourage your child to change his printing into the book type. Explain to him that he is to print one way and books can use another type of printing.

Phonics: Sound of *ce* and *ge*

Tell your student that the letter *c* he has been using at the first of the word followed by *o* or *a* or *u* has been the hard-sounding *c*. It sounds more like *k* than *c* (*coat, cake, cute*). Now he is going to think of another sound for *c*. It is soft like the hissing sound *s* can make. When *c* is soft it chooses the letter *e* to stand next to it. The *e* is shaped like *c*, only it has that crossbar. Have your student print *ce, ce, ce*, on lined paper. If he has a typewriter, he can type the *ce* pattern. There are several layer-cake words with *ce*. He can decode: *face, lace, race, dice, rice, nice*. Then he can print these words from dictation. (He can type them also.)

Tell your student that usually when *g* has *e* after it, the hard *g* sound turns to a soft sound (*gate*–hard, *page*–soft). He says that soft sound of *g* when he is disappointed and says, "Oh, gee." (He will just drop off the *ee* sound.) The soft *g* in layer-cake words: *cage, page, rage, sage, wage*. (You will have to explain the meaning of *wage* and *sage*.)

Extra Words

Several of the Extra Words will be integrated into the phonics as the program progresses. By this time, your student has seen the word *in* many times. Can he read it by sight? You may think that a tiny word like that would be easy but to many people, two-letter words all look very much alike. Give your student the sound of the short *i* in the word *in*.

It may help if you place a picture of an Indian with the word *in* of the word Indian underlined. Your pupil may need to associate the beginning sound of Indian with words like *in*. However, you need to point out that the *I* of Indian is capitalized. Do not stress the fact that you are using short vowels. Place the following words on cards. Hang them around the house. Ask every once in a while for the sound of *i* in these short words: *in, if, it, is*.

You also need to state that *s* sometimes has another sound besides the hissing one. It is a buzzing *z* sound. The word *is* has that *z* sound. Have your pupil decode the *s* sound in: *nose, rose, hose, pose, wise, fuse*. Dictate these words for your student to print. Start the next lesson if there is time.

WORD LIST

bean	bean	**huge**	huge
beam	beam	**gain**	gain
gear	gear	**gate**	gate
goat	goat	**pail**	pail
goal	goal	**gave**	gave

SILLY SENTENCES

1. Joan has a nice face.
2. Jake would like to race.
3. The mice eat rice.
4. Could Jane have lace on the cape?
5. The game has dice.

1. The mice like the cage.
2. Joan can read page nine.
3. The mule is in a rage.
4. He is paid a wage.

LESSON 33

Phonics: *old, ild* patterns

There are some sets of words that have long vowels but do not have that second silent vowel. By introducing these special words at this time the student gets used to them before he has to learn that in one-vowel, one-syllable words the vowel is usually short. Explain that the letters *ld* make *o* and *i* have a long sound even though they have no silent friend to join them. Your student can decode: *cold, bold, fold, gold, hold, mold, old, wild, mild.*

SILLY SENTENCES

1. The old bold toad liked the cold cave.

2. Can Joad hold the gold?

3. The wild mule could hide in the cave.

4. Can he fold the coat?

5. Dave feels a mild fear.

6. The wild boar can leap into the air.

7. The team can wait in the mild rain.

8. Would he hold the cold meat?

9. The meat has mold on it.

10. Would he like mold on the meat?

LESSON 34

Extra Words

Your pupil has learned the long *o* sound. You can now tell him *o* has another sound. He is to use the following words: *or, on.* These words will be used in the stories often, so that if you keep helping him he will learn them by sight. (You do not have to drill this new *o* sound, short *o*. Later he will come to see that *o* words with only one vowel will have this sound.)

Phonics: Review of long *e*

Each day try to see that the child covers the following areas.

1. Review the Extra Words.
2. Read the Word List.
3. Read the story. (Be sure to follow the Seven Special Steps).
4. Student prints six to ten words that you dictate. (Always ask what vowel he hears in the word before he starts to print. Then what is the first letter, etc.)
5. The Game can be played.

These items can be done in one session or in separate sessions each day.

This lesson is a review of the peanut butter and jelly pattern of words. Review the instructions in Lesson 29 on the comparison of the two structures. Have your student reread the Word List and the Silly Sentences in Lessons 17 and 19.

LESSON 35

Phonics: Layer-cake and sandwich words

Have your student look at the two Word Lists in this lesson. Can he tell you which are peanut butter and jelly sandwich words and which are the layer-cake words with *e* frosting? Praise his success enthusiastically. Ask him if he realizes how much he has learned. He really has worked hard. Now point at random to some of the words for him to read. You can cut out pictures of a sandwich and a layer cake from a magazine. Put the pictures in front of your student. Mix up a number of the cards you have printed with the two types of words; let your pupil place the correct type of word on the right picture (one word on each card). Then select words from each list for a written spelling test. If your student hesitates over each word, you can tell him whether it is a layer-cake or a peanut butter and jelly word. Do not be discouraged if your student reads better than he spells. Do *not* give negative criticism. Spelling skill always lags behind reading skill. Pleasantly remind your student that there is still need for more review.

Remember: Peanut Butter and Jelly Words

slice of bread = consonant ⎫
crunchy peanut butter =
long vowel   ⎬ soak
jelly = silent vowel
slice of bread = consonant ⎭

Remember: Layer-Cake Words

layer cake = consonant ⎫
strawberry frosting = long
vowel.   ⎬ make
layer cake = consonant
e frosting = silent *e* ⎭

Following the Word Lists in this lesson are words to be identified. The student is to put a dash after the peanut butter and jelly words and a round dot after the layer-cake words. (Have him associate the round dot with the round layer cake.) The dyslexic or the student with a short attention span may be able to tell you the difference between the words but be unable to remember how to use the dot or dash. If you find he is troubled, have him make the identification and you place the signals: a dash for peanut butter and jelly words and a dot for the layer-cake words.

114

WORD LIST
Peanut Butter and Jelly Words

boat			bail	bait	
coal	coat		fail		
foam			jail		
goal	goat		hail	hair	
load	loaf		main	maid	mail
moan			pail	pair	
Joan			rain	rail	raid
road	roam	roar	sail		
soap	soak		tail		
toad					

beef	beet		bead	beat	bean
deer			deal	dear	Dean
feet	feel		fear		
keep			gear		
heel			heat	heal	hear
need			leaf	leap	leak
meet			meal	mean	meat
peep			neat	near	
seed	seem	seek	peak		
week	weed		read	real	

→

WORD LIST

Layer-Cake Words

bone				bake	base		
cone	cove	coke		cake	cape	cane	came
dome				date	dare	Dave	
hole	home	hope		face	fame	fade	
lone				gate	game	gave	
joke				hate			
more	mole			Jake	Jane		
note	nose			lake	lane	lame	late
pole	poke			make	mate	made	
tone				name			
rope	rose			pave	pale		
sore				rate	rake		
zone				sale	save	same	

bike	bite			cute	cube	cure
dime	dine			fuse		
fire	fine	five		huge		
hide	hike	hive		mule		
kite						
lime	line	life				
mile	mine	mice	Mike			
nice						
pile	pipe	pine				
ride	rice					
side	size					
tide	time					

→

WORD LIST

Layer-Cake and Peanut Butter and Jelly Words

bean	soap	seam
hail	meal	soak
hole	tide	wine
pail	nose	home
bone	sail	weed
coal	heel	hose
nail	time	weep
tide	fear	main
more	seed	gear
tone	hope	ripe
team	dome	lime
rail	read	leak
rice	pore	raid
tone	weed	pine
zone	vine	lone

LESSON 36

Phonics: Capital *B* and *R*

Two new capital letters can be given, *B* and *R*. Capital *B* starts like capital *P*; it just adds another bulge underneath. Capital *R* starts like capital *B* but does not act the same in the bottom square. It has a diagonal line like capital *N*.

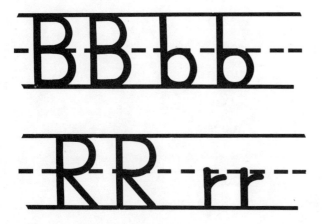

Extra Words

You will read *at* and *that* for the student in his Silly Story. Put these words on cards in the Extra Word envelope. Soon you will explain about this *a* sound when you add *as, am, an*.

Words with *ough* often create great problems. *Ough* can acquire *six* different sounds. If you introduce each group carefully, the student responds well. In this lesson you will work with *rough* and *tough*.

Tell your student that he has used *ou* in the word *would* and now he will use these two letters again. The sound will be different. Again, it will not sound like either *o* or *u* but like *a* when you say, "I have *a* kite." Have your student print *ou, ou* several times (they can be typed, too), then show him how **g** with his tail likes to have tall *h* sit beside him. The tall line of *h* sticks up to balance **g**'s long tail. Have your pupil print *gh, gh, gh*. Now have him start with *ou* and add *gh*. Then repeat *ough* several times. By putting *t* or *r* in front, two words are made. They rhyme with *puff*. Tell your pupil that he will meet *gh* many times. It may have the sound of *f* or it might be silent! Put these two words on cards in surprise places around the house.

SILLY STORY

The Rough Brute

I could see a tough brute pile five toads into my boat near my home. The tough brute could take a huge load in that boat. One toad would dive into the lake, then the rough brute put more toads into the boat.

The tough brute gave a huge roar and a huge moan. The load of toads in the boat gave a dive into the lake. The rough brute would rage at the tame toads that dared to dive from the boat.

In a rage the rough brute would take a pair of toads and put the toads in a pail. The toads gave a dive into the lake. The toads tried to leap clear of the rough tough brute. In time the tough rough brute gave up.

Feed Words: up, my, from, clear, brute, then, put.

LESSON 37

Phonics: Capital letters A, D, M, H, T, G

Capital *A* is like a teepee. Your student starts at the middle top of his box, then he pulls his line down to the left corner (under the hand that holds the paper). He goes back to the top where he started again and heads down for the other corner. He finishes with a line across the middle of the teepee.

Capital letter *D* starts with a straight line on the left side of the box. Your pupil then returns to the top of that line, swings away ("Good-bye, hand") down and across the bottom.

D is a difficult capital letter for some children because the round part of the capital involves a reversal process. The capital *D* has the reverse curve of the small *d*. Do *not* tell your pupil that small *d* and big *D* go in opposite directions because then in the future he has to try to remember the direction each letter takes. Just tell him small *d* starts as *c* whereas big capital *D* starts as a straight line and branches out like the side part of the letter *h*. Then it comes down and tucks under.

M starts just like capital *D*. A straight line down the side. Now a straight line down the other side of the box. (Always insist that your pupil draw the straight line on the left side first. Thirteen capital letters start with left-side straight lines.)

Now he will put a small letter *v* in the top of the box between the two straight lines.

Capital letter *H* has two straight lines like *M* only the *v* is replaced with a horizontal line across the middle.

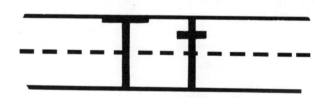

The capital letter *T* just puts the crosspiece at the top.

Capital *G* is different from the small one. The letter is just like capital *C* with a tabletop resting on the bottom curl.

You have noticed that I did not introduce capital letters immediately. I stated before that the letters that are introduced in this book are actually review work. Again I state that this book is for the student who has had previous (even though unsuccessful) exposure to letter shapes and sounds.

You can introduce the capital letter shapes as they are needed. Twelve of the letters have the same shape as their lower-case form, only they must fill the full space between two solid lines. These letters are: C, K, O, P, S, T, U, V, W, X, Y, Z. The crossbar of capital T is moved up to the top of the straight line. The bottom of capital P and Y sit on the floor line. They do not drop below the line like small p and y.

Each day you can dictate two of the sentences listed at the end of this section in order to give your student practice in starting a sentence with a capital letter.

When your student meets the rest of the capitals that have not already been introduced, you can refer to this lesson. Each of the capital letters will fill the full space between two lines. Capital F looks much like small f, but the top is square. E is like F with a bottom line. You will be challenged to find some way to help your student associate the relationship of capital E with small e.

Big L just adds that bottom line that wants to point to the next letter to be written. Big H is two straight lines with the crossbar. It really looks like small h but with an additional line on the upper right-hand side.

Capital M is two straight lines with a small v in the upper center section. Capital G is like C with a tabletop resting across the last point you make. Capital G's beginning shape is just like small g only it fills a bigger space.

Capital D is difficult for two reasons. It can be reversed easily and it just does not look like small d. To avoid problems, I make sure my pupils are very familiar with making capital L with its bottom line reaching forward to be right beside the next letter to be formed. I have my students make capital L, then swing that floor line up to the top of where L started   These directives are for the dyslexic person who has directional problems.

Capital N is two straight lines. The diagonal starts at the top of the first line and reaches down to the bottom of the second line. N does not look like small n. You have to use your ingenuity to make an association for your pupil. The same situation applies for capital A. A is a teepee with its crossbar. I do not teach capital Q until the *qu* words are introduced.

These instructions leave you with the responsibility of deciding when you should work with capitals. Do *not* teach them all at once!

Sentences for dictation using capital letters:

1. Craig likes the cake.
2. Be nice to Kate.
3. Take the tea to Joan.
4. Pile the foam in the pail.
5. See the soap.
6. The tea is nice.
7. Use the cute kite.
8. You can see the goat.
9. Wait here.
10. Oak leaves can soak in the pail.

TWO: CONSONANT BLENDS WITH LONG VOWELS

LESSON 38

Extra Words

Review. Add the word *too*. Explain to your student that he will find out there are three words that say *to*. Each one is spelled differently and there are three separate meanings. The word *to* shows direction. When an extra *o* is added, the word seems to have too much hitched to it. The word means more than you need. Do *not* at this time explain that the word *too* can mean *also*. (The third *two* will be used later.)

Phonics: Consonant blends *bl, br*

The directions for this next unit seem lengthy. Once you read them carefully, you will find they will apply to the rest of the lessons in this unit.

In the previous lessons, most of the words have long vowels combined with separate *single* consonants. In this new unit you will introduce a group of letters called consonant blends. A consonant blend is a combination of two or more consonants whose sounds blur together.

When you read the list of words on the phonics Word List, you will realize how you use blends all the time. Turn to the Word List which precedes this lesson; it is not an exercise page. Use it to show your student what interesting patterns the words he speaks can make when printed. Look how neat the list is — *bl, br, cl, cr, fl, fr, gl, gr, pl, pr*. Ask your student to stop there. Ask him what happened to *dl*. Can he think of any word that starts out with *dl?* Help him look in the dictionary. Would you believe it? We do not have one word that starts with *dl*. Try and blend the two letters together. They do not work!

The lessons in this section include the words that have blends combined with *long vowels*. (Notice *ch, sh, th*, etc., are not blends. These are two consonants together, but they have only one sound. They are called digraphs. You will work with digraphs later.)

Some students' auditory perception has not fully developed or may be faulty. Often when these students hear the *bl, cl, gl*, etc., they transfer this sound into the visual picture of *bul, cul*, etc., and they transfer *br, cr*, to *bir* or *bur*, or *cur*. If your child has been exposed to concentrated emphasis in short vowels at a too early stage, this blending confusion takes place.

Do not have the child read the words on the Word List for *bl, br,* until he has practiced the first column of exercise sounds.

Just work first with *bl* combined with each long vowel. This is extremely difficult for some children. Be patient and show good humor. Say to your child, "Isn't it amazing what tricks our brain, ears, and eyes play on us? Nothing seems to want to go together. Don't worry, soon you will think back and wonder what was so hard. Remember how hard that first lesson was? Now those words seem easy."

Be sure to have your student repeat the vowel aloud before he tries to combine it with the consonant blend (*bl*). After reading these exercises in the first column (just the *bl*), dictate these sounds for your student to print. If you have a typewriter, have him practice *bl*, space, *bl*, space, several times then dictate *bla*. Can he tell you what he should type? He may give you the wrong vowel. Patiently (with fun in your voice) repeat the sound with strong emphasis on the vowel. Then ask what he hears. Occasionally a child will be so apprehensive nothing comes out right. Do not consider that the lesson is too hard. Just realize you should change over to a review lesson. Tackle his new lesson later in the day or tomorrow.

If all is going well, your student first prints, then types *bla, ble, bli,* and *blo.* He can then try decoding the full words in the second column. If all of this work has been extremely easy, you can continue with *br.* Otherwise take the *br* tomorrow. After the work with the Word List has been completed, follow the usual directions for the Silly Stories.

Explain to your pupil that these consonant blends *bl, br,* etc., act like one big fat slice of bread or layer cake. He will find the same peanut butter and jelly words as well as the layer-cake kind. Can he find them for you? Have your pupil decode the following words.

WORD LISTS

bl	blade		pr	pride
br	brave		sl	slate
cl	claim		sm	smile
cr	crate		sn	snail
dr	drain		sc	scale
fl	flake		sk	skate
fr	frame		st	state
gl	glare		sw	sweet
gr	grade		tr	trail
pl	plane		tw	tweet

bla	blade	blame	blare	blaze
ble	bleed	bleak	bleat	
bra	brace	brave	braid	brain
bre	breeze			
bri	bride	brine		
bro	broke			

SILLY STORY

Brave Brian

Brave Brian could feel a wild breeze in the air. Brave Brian like<u>d</u> the wild breeze. It would be nice to sail his boat in the wild breeze.

Brave Brian said he would take his cute bride to sail in the wild breeze. Brave Brian<u>'s</u> cute bride like<u>d</u> the sail in the wild breeze.

The wild breeze would lean on the sail and pile the boat on it<u>s</u> side. The cute bride could brace herself in the seat. All of a sudden the mean breeze <u>be</u>came too wild. The rope to hold the sail broke.

Brave Brian did not feel too nice. Brave Brian would take the blame for the wild ride.

Brave Brian<u>'s</u> cute bride said she did not care. The wild ride made the day seem fine.

Feed Words: herself, all, sudden, did, for.

LESSON 39

Extra Words

Review *would, could, the, they, a, to, do, and, in, if, it, is, at, as, am, an.* By adding *c* to *an* your student can decode the word *can.*

Phonics: Consonant blends *cl, cr* and the question mark and quotation marks

Place before your student the following cards: *coat, cake, cute.* Keep reviewing the following facts: the letter *c* sounds like the sound of *k* when it sits in front of round *o* or round *a* that leans on a stick or *u* that is not round at the top. Now *c* is going to have that hard sound when he sits in front of tall stick letter *l*. Have your student repeat the *cl* sound as in *claim,* several times. Have him print (type, also) *cl, cl,* then *claim, clean.* Follow the above procedure for *cr* using the words *creep, creek.* (Explain that a creek is a small river.) Your pupil may want to print *c* for the last letter in *creek.* Tell him *c* is too wide open to stay at the end of a word. (Do not be upset if your student forgets when to use hard or soft letter sounds. This concept takes a long time to digest. You just have to keep patiently repeating the information.)

Ask your child to look at the marks at the end of the sentences in a magazine or newspaper. If he has not learned to identify a question mark and a period, now is the time to teach him.

Tell your student that the dot is a period. It goes at the end of the group of words that tell you something. Sometimes you want to ask a question. Then you put a special mark on top of a period. This is called a question mark. Have the child print a mark like the round part of the letter *p*, ˀ . Then your pupil can put a tail on it with a dot underneath. (If he gets confused he can make the letter *p* and erase the upper part of the straight line ? .)

Now you can explain quotation marks. State that when people speak to each other, the only way we can realize this on the printed page is by putting what we call quotation marks at the top of the sentence at the beginning and end. The words before this kind of sentence have to be, *he said,* or *she said,* etc. These words tell us if someone is speaking. Point to the quotation marks in the story. Later you can have your student print sentences with punctuation.

WORD LIST

cla	claim	Claire		
cle	clean	clear		
clo	close	cloak		
cra	crane	crate	crave	Craig
cre	creek	cream	creep	crease
cro	croak			
dra	drain	drape	drake	
dri	drive			
dre	dream			
dro	drove	drone		

SILLY STORY

Claire Bride

Claire Bride claim<u>ed</u> she would hire the tough rough brute to clean the mule.

Mule said, "Claire Bride, I <u>re</u>fuse to be clean<u>ed</u> by the rough tough brute."

Claire Bride said, "Mule, you need to be clean so I can ride you. It would be a crime, if you would not like to be clean."

Mule said, "I do not care if it would be a crime to <u>re</u>fuse to be clean. I hate the rough tough brute. You can <u>not</u> blame me, if I do <u>not</u> <u>re</u>main clean. Would you like to be clean<u>ed</u> by a tough rough brute?"

Feed Words: by, not, you, brute, said.

LESSON 40

Extra Words

Review *would, could, to, do, too, the, they, and, a, in, if, it, is*. Explain that *did* has the same vowel sound as *i* in *it*. Can your student decode *did?* Always point to the vowel, have him repeat it aloud, then proceed.

You can also print the word *the*, cross out *e*, reprint *th* and add the word *at*. Have him decode *that*.

Add the word *mother*. You have already introduced the sound *th* by using the words *that, they*. Print the word *mother* on a card. Underline *th*. Point to this pattern. Ask what that sound is. Then pronounce the whole word. You may have to feed this word each time. Usually, however, the child has been exposed to the word *mother* so many times that it is not new to him.

Phonics: Consonant blend *dr*

Follow previous lesson instructions using *dr*. Use the Word List in Lesson 39.

SILLY STORY

A Dream

At night I had a dream that I could drive a bike on the floor at home. In the dream I drove and drove over the floor.

In the dream I drove into the door. Then I woke up.

When I woke up, I could see that I did not drive on the floor at home. I am sure mother would not like me to ride the bike on the floor.

Feed Words: floor, up, sure, when, not, over, on, then.

LESSON 41

Extra Words

Do you have the Extra Words in a special envelope? Review them. Keep making more cards using the new Word Lists. Your student loves to play The Game.

Phonics: The sound of y and consonant blends fl, fr

Print the following words on cards: *my, by, cry, fry.* Tell your student that when *y* is the last letter of a word, it does strange things. It may stay silent, as in *day,* or it may changes its sound. In these tiny words, the *y* takes on the *i* sound. Each time you come to a lesson with one of these words, print the word and ask your student what sound that *y* changes to. (I erase the right side line of the *y* and put a dot on what is left:

Then I say, "Maybe that is where that *i* sound comes from, even though *i* is tipped over!")

It is *very* important to keep asking your pupil to tell you when he meets these words what the letter *y* does. This is training that will help the student avoid spelling problems later. People with poor visual memories have to depend on sounds when spelling. Our English language can be complicated if these variations in spelling are not taught in simplified form with much repetition. (Some teachers assume that poor visual memory means lack of intelligence. Do not fall into this trap.)

Follow the usual procedure for the Word List and the Silly Stories.

WORD LIST

fla	flake	flame	flare
fle	fleet		
flo	float	floor	
fra	frame		
free	free	freeze	freak
fro	froze		

SILLY STORY

A Snow Flake

If I had a snow flake, I would try to save it. It would be nice to put my snow flake in a frame. If I froze my snow flake, would it remain in the frame? No, my snow flake would not stay frozen in a frame. I would have to keep the snow flake from a flame, too. I could not fry my snow flake, could I?

Feed Words: snow, from, had, put, no, have, stay, not.

LESSON 42

Extra Words

Review *would, could, do, to, too, and, a, mother, in, if, it, is, did, at, as, am, an, the, they, that.*

Add the words *then* and *when.* Explain that *en* sounds just like the alphabet name of *n.* Your student can read the word *the* and add the alphabet letter sound *n* and come up with the full word *then.* He will make the adjustment in the whole-word sound once he decodes it.

Remind your pupil of the tongue and lip positions of *th.* Show him how to shape his lips and blow for *wh.* (His tongue can rest on the floor of his mouth.) Then he can add *en.*

Phonics: Review of consonant blends *fl, fr, dr*

You will need to explain that a boy duck is called a drake. Teach the lesson as usual.

SILLY STORY

Craig, the Drake

Joan has a nice clean drake named Craig. The nice clean drake named Craig became frail. At night the lake would freeze. So clean Craig, the drake, almost froze. He became so frail he could not creep.

Joan cried. She could not be brave. Joan cried when she would see the frail drake.

Dr. Kane came by. He said to Joan, "Craig, the drake, has the flu. We can make the drake feel fine. We should feed Craig a pile of fine seeds."

Joan said, "Dr. Kane, I will keep a fire beside the lake. Craig, my drake, should sleep near the flame of the fire. Then he will feel fine."

Feed Words: almost, not, should, has, will, Dr., she, night, has, of, sleep.

LESSON 43

Extra Words

Your pupil should be able to recognize the word *as* when he sees it in a sentence. Have him print *as*. Ask if he can now print *has*. Repeat the word with a heavy emphasis on the *as*, then again with a heavy emphasis on the *h*. Now can he print *had*, then *have?* Explain that when the sound of *s* and soft *c* can be heard at the end of words, *e* loves to follow. The letter *v* never wants to be the last letter. If the sound of *v* is at the end of the word, *e* will follow; *save, dive, have.*

Phonics: Consonant blends *gl, gr*

Follow the regular procedure. Do not forget to have the student print (and type) a few of the words after he decodes the list of words in each lesson. You may help him by telling him ahead of time that the word is a layer-cake or peanut butter and jelly form. If your student has a poor visual memory you can see why the spelling is difficult. Even if he prints the letters correctly from their sounds, the word can be wrong. Repetition and little clues he can make for himself save your pupil if you help him review often enough.

WORD LIST

gla	glade	glare	glaze	
gle	gleam			
gli	glide			
glo	gloat			
gra	grade	grave	graze	grain
gre	greed	green	greet	grease
gri	grime	gripe		
gro	groan	grove		

SILLY STORIES

Grease and Grime

Grease and grime make me groan. I like to see my home gleam with a clean shine. It would make my face gleam in a huge smile if my home could be free from grease and grime.

Feed Words: with, shine, smile, from.

Grace and Grapes

Grace would like a nice grape vine near her home. Grace would feel fine if she had a nice seat beside a grape vine. Grace would eat the grapes when she had her tea.

Feed Words: her, she.

139

LESSON 44

Extra Words

Add the word *his*. Show your pupil the card with the word *is*. Have him print *is*, then add *h*. If your child uses the typewriter, have him type *is*, space, *is*, space, several times, then he can type *h*, space, *h*, space, across the paper. On the next line he can type *his*, space, *his*, space, etc. Can he read the word after he types it? You would think that after spelling and typing the word, of course your student could read it. However, your pupil has been using a different brain pathway from that used for reading. He may have to be helped through the word by using the Seven Special Steps. (Do not repeat it for him.)

Phonics: Consonant blends *pl, pr*

Introduce the *pl* and *pr* sound. If your child has been exposed to phonics in school and has had to struggle with short vowels before he has met these consonant blends (*bl, br, cl, dr,* etc.), he may be visualizing in his mind the wrong letter pattern. He may think *pl* is *pul* and *pr* is *pur* or even *par*. If he is confused, turn back to the first Word List at the start of the consonant blends. Show your child that neat pattern of *bl, br, cl, cr, fl, fr, gl, gr, pl, pr* (do not go further). Ask your child to print some nonsense words for you (words that do not mean anything): *bla, bro, clo, cre, fla, fra, gli, gri, ple, pri*. He may surprise you and print *blai* (this, of course, is acceptable). Continue the lesson by having your child read the Word List. If his attention has been stretched to the limit, leave the story for the next session.

The child has to use his imagination about the details of these stories. The limited vocabulary makes the descriptions rather vague. Encourage the child to talk about the parts that are left out. Ask your child where he thinks that plate of prunes was. Maybe a picnic table was near. Maybe the dining room window was open.

The words *plain* and *plane* are homonyms. You will need to explain that we have many of these words that sound the same but are spelled differently and have different meanings, such as *pale–pail; beet–beat; weak–week;* etc.

WORD LIST

pla	plane	plain	plate	play
ple	plead	please		
pra	pray			
pri	prime	price	pride	
pro	probe			

SILLY STORY

The Plain Gray Airplane

Pete liked to play with his nice plain gray airplane. At times he played on the floor with his nice plain gray airplane.

Pete seemed to feel a fine pride for his nice plane.

One day Pete said he would fly the nice plain gray airplane up in the sky.

He waved the plain gray airplane into the air. The breeze would not hold the plain gray airplane up in the air. Where did it land? Right in a plate of prunes!

Feed Words: with, where, prunes.

LESSON 45

Phonics: Silent *gh* with long *i*

Previous lessons may need extra review days. At any point when you think too much information is piling up on your child, go back and review earlier stories.

Let the child draw pictures about the stories. Show enthusiasm for the drawings. Do not correct the child's artwork. Be sure you keep rewarding the child when he reaches specific goals.

The pattern *gh* is not a consonant blend. However, this lesson is tucked in at this point because the words in this *ight* group are helpful for sentence building.

The child has met *gh* in the group of letters *ough*. The *gh* changed into the *f* sound in the *ough*. In this lesson tell the child that the *gh* in the *ight* is just stuck in to trap him. See if he can fool those words and show them he can remember that *gh* is silent.

You will need to make a set of cards using the Word List of this lesson. Print the first two letters in black. Print the *gh* in yellow, then print the *t* in black. The child sees that the *gh* seems to fade out. It becomes silent. (These words have long *i* but no second silent vowel. Your student will meet a few sets of words of this nature.)

WORD LIST

fight   light   might   night   right   bright   flight   fright

SILLY SENTENCES

1. Grace would like to take a flight in a plane.
2. At night the light is not bright.
3. It is not right to fight.
4. Craig would not fight a snake.
5. He came at the right time.

LESSONS 46 and 47

Extra Words

Add the word *not*. You have used this word so often as a Feed Word your child may now be able to recognize it. If he does not know it, print the word *no*. Tell him that if he adds the letter *t* to the word *no*, the sound of the *o* cannot be its alphabet name because it has to have two vowels to give it the long sound. (Along with two or more consonants.) Therefore, the word *no* changes into *not*. (Actually this *o* is short *o*. Your student will see the logic of the word later.) Repetition will help anchor the word.

Phonics: Consonant blends *sl, sm, sn*

This Word List that follows will be used for two separate lessons. You will need to spend a few days on each part. Follow your usual procedure. Use the *sl* pattern with its stories. Then use the *sm* and *sn* pattern for the next lesson along with the Silly Story, *Sneak, the Snake*. Most students like to make pictures of Sneak, the snake. Continue making new cards with the new words for The Game.

Sentences to print from dictation: When you dictate a long-vowel word, always ask what vowel the student hears. Then ask if he can remember if the word is a peanut butter and jelly word or a layer-cake word with silent *e* frosting.

1. I like the slice of meat.
2. I slide in the sleet.
3. He could sleep in the cave.

1. Sneak, the snake, is in the shade.
2. Can Sneak, the snake, sneeze?
3. Can a snail smile?

1. The slice of meat is nice.
2. I slide on the slope.
3. I smile at the snake.

WORD LIST

sla	slate	slave	
sli	slide	slice	sly
slo	slope		
sle	sleek	sleep	sleet	sleeve
sme	smear		
smi	smile		
smo	smoke		
sna	snail		
sne	sneak	sneeze	
sno	snore		
spe	speed		

SILLY STORIES

My Snail

One day my snail gave more of a sneeze than you would feel he could. What do you feel would take place if a snail sneeze<u>d</u>?

You are right. The <u>in</u>side of the snail came out!

Feed Words: out, are, than, what.

→

SILLY STORIES

My Sleek, Sly Snail

My sleek, sly, snail likes to slide in the sand. At times the slime makes my sleek, sly, snail slide on the slope.

The sand is like sleet for the snail. If sleet freezes on slate I slide on it. So I should see that my sleek, sly, snail could slide on slime or sand or sleet.

Feed Words: for, sand, should.

Sneak, the Snake

Sneak, the snake, would doze in the shade of a tree. In his sleep Sneak, the snake, had a dream that he had to soak in slime.

The sight of the green slime gave Sneak, the snake, a pain. When he woke up he smiled. He could see he did not have to soak in the slime.

With speed he poked his way into a place where he could hide. Sneak, the snake, would like to slide into the road, when Peter drove by on his bike.

What a fright he would give Pete!

Feed Words: with, where, what.

LESSON 48

Phonics: *Should, ill* group and consonant blend *st*

Your student has used the words *would* and *could* many times. Show him how you can replace the first consonant with *sh* to make *should*. Explain that in consonant blends you can really hear each letter but there is a group of two-letter patterns that create a new sound that is not like either of the letters. He has already been using two in this group, *th* and *gh* (these are called digraphs, if you want to use the word). The combination *sh* fits in this group. The two letters make a sound quite different from *s* or *h*. You make the sound when you tell someone to be quiet.

Another word to add to the list that does not have a long vowel is *will*. Here is short *i* that your pupil has been using in the words *in, it, is, if.* Now he can decode the *ill* group of words. Always have him vocalize the vowel sound before he starts the list.

In this lesson with the consonant blend *st*, your student meets the word *pie*. Here is a new two-vowel combination that follows the rule: first vowel says its name, second vowel must be silent.

Print the *ill* group of words on cards. Explain that the sound of *i* is like the *i* in the word *in*. Play The Game with these cards. Dictate the sentences.

The *ill* group: *Bill, dill, fill, hill, Jill, kill, mill, pill, will, still, drill, frill, grill.*

Sentences for dictation:

1. Bill will drill a hole in the grill.
2. Bill still can fill the hole.
3. Jill and Bill will stay on the hill.
4. Jill will fill the pail.

WORD LIST

sta	state	stale	stain	stay
sto	stone	stole	stove	store
ste	steam	steep	steal	

SILLY STORY

Stale Pie

Pete's mother said, "Pete, this pie is stale."

"Go to the store keeper and say I will not keep this stale pie. I can make a pie in my stove that will not be stale."

Pete rode on his bike to the store on a steep road. When Pete got to the store, Pete could see the store keeper on the chair, asleep. Pete gave the man a poke.

Pete said, "Mr. Store Keeper, why did you make my mother buy a stale pie?"

The man woke up and then he said, "I did not make your mother buy a stale pie. While I snored a tough dope smeared prunes on the pie. The prunes made the pie taste stale."

The store keeper said, "I should pay your mother for the pie." And he did.

Feed Words: why, buy, up, while, your, chair, for, Mr., prunes.

LESSON 49

Extra Words

At the beginning of the book you started special envelopes. You now should have *a, e, i, o, u, oa, ai, ee, ea* in your Long Vowel envelope. There is quite an assortment in your Extra Word envelope. Take a new envelope and label it Short *i*. Put in these cards, *it, if, is, in, did*. Then make cards for the *ill* group to be placed in with the short *i* words. Label another envelope Short *o*. Put in the cards *on, not*. The next envelope will be Short *e*; add the cards *then, when*. The Short *a* envelope will have *at, that, as, has, had, have, am, an, can, than, and*.

All you have left for the Extra Word envelope is *would, could, should, mother, a, to, too, do, rough, tough*. You can add *put*. To help your student memorize this word, you can place cards with *put* printed on them in various spots around the house. Your student has only eleven words he has to remember by sight.

Phonics: Consonant blend *str*

Your pupil will now meet a three-letter consonant blend. It combines the *st* of the previous lesson with the letter *r*. Proceed with your routine. Be sure to select a few words from the list for spelling words, after your student has practiced printing (and typing) the *str* pattern. You now have had enough experience teaching to think of original ideas to help your child with the other blends.

Your pupil has used the word *and* many times. He can decode the *and* group on the Word List.

When your student hesitates over the sound of the short vowel words, you can repeat the vowel sound for him, then let him finish with the decoding.

WORD LIST

Consonant blend *str*

stra	strain	stray	
stri	stripe	strike	
stro	stroke		
stre	street	streak	stream

Consonant blends *sk, sc, sw, tw*

ska	skate	
sca	scale	scare
scre	scream	
scro	scroll	
swe	sweet	
twe	tweet	

The *and* group

and	band	sand	land
hand	stand	grand	brand
bland	gland	strand	

SILLY STORY

Jane Gave a Scream

Jake like<u>s</u> to take a walk <u>be</u>side sweet Jane. They like to walk on the street by the stream.

One day a stray tame deer came up to sweet Jane. Jane gave a scream. The scream scare<u>d</u> the tame deer. He gave a leap and land<u>ed</u> in the stream.

The stream seem<u>ed</u> as cold as froze<u>n</u> ice. The tame deer did not stay in the cold stream. Like a streak he made a leap and splash<u>ed</u> from the stream.

Sweet Jane said she could weep. She did not mean to scare the tame deer.

Feed Words: one, up, from, said, she.

THREE: VOWEL INTEGRALS

LESSON 50

Phonics: The long *o* sound of *ough*

You have taught the sound of *ough* in the words *tough* and *rough*. Now you are to work with the *ough* having the sound of long *o*, as in the words *dough, doughnut, though,* and *although.* Explain to your student that he has learned the pronunciation of the word *do,* now he is going to meet a group of words where the *o* in *do* is given a long *o* sound. The rest of the *ugh* is silent. Where do you suppose we ever dug this word up?

Before the child reads the story, have him print *ough,* then *dough* four times. The *d* should be one color, the *ough* pattern another color. Have the child put a long mark over the *o* the same color as the *d.* However, the pattern of *ough* should remain one color. (Later, he meets four other sounds of *ough!* — *cough, enough, bough, through.*) Most doughnut shops shorten the word to donut. You can point this out to your student. You can ask your student to look at a donut sign and ask what is left out. Most students will *not* be able to tell you. You have been teaching the child to recognize letter patterns that have become special points he focuses on. He now looks at the word to see first-vowel, second-vowel patterns. However, when you ask him to tell you what is missing in the word *donut,* you are asking him to perform an entirely different skill from what he has been doing daily. This new skill can be acquired at a later date when your child's neurological development progresses.

SILLY STORY

Pie Dough

Have you seen Mother make a pie? She rolls the dough on a board. She rolls the dough thin. Then she puts the dough in a pie plate. She puts in grapes. Then Mother folds dough to put on the grapes.

Although grape pie may be nice, I do not like grape pie. I do like the pie dough my mother makes, though. Mother's dough is not tough!

LESSON 51

Phonics: Diphthongs *oi, oy*

A diphthong is a vowel or a group of vowels producing two speech sounds in a one-syllable word or in a syllable. (This definition is for your use only.)

In the next few lessons, the diphthongs will be introduced. The auditory perception of your child is not highly developed enough for him to grasp the fine points of some of the combinations. However, because the child uses the words in his conversation he can manage the words successfully.

You can explain the *oi* and *oy* sound as starting to be a long *o* sound slurring into a long *e* sound.

The diphthongs *ou* and *ow* in this section will have the sound of the *ou* and *ow* in *house* and *cow*.

The *oo* and *ew* will have the sound as in *moon* and *flew*.

NOTE: Help your student with the *ing* ending. Remember there are words in the stories your student will not understand. The word *cease* is not used in conversation very often, therefore an explanation is due.

WORD LIST

boy	oil	join
toy	noise	coin
joy	spoil	joint
	toil	point
	boil	
	foil	
	coil	
	soil	
	broil	

SILLY STORY

Roy and His Voice

Roy could make his voice make a noise that would scare a giant.

One night Roy seemed sure he could hear a wild noise. The noise seemed to be in the soil under his feet. Could there be a huge hole under his feet?

Roy seemed to be scared. Then Roy said, "I should not be scared. I should make my voice make a noise that would scare that wild dope under the soil. I am not going to have that noise under the soil spoil my day."

So Roy, the boy, screamed with his voice. Then he made a noise with his voice that seemed like boiling oil.

After that Roy ceased to hear a peep from the hole under the soil.

Feed Words: there, under, after, sure, said, with.

LESSON 52

Phonics: The ar and *end* pattern

Explain to your student that when he meets *ar* he must look quickly to see if the letter *e* follows (*care, dare*). If it does not, then the sound is going to be the same as the alphabet name of the letter *r:* the letter *a* has to be quiet and let *r* speak his name.

These *ar* words may not be difficult for your student. However, when he meets the *er, ir, ur* patterns, trouble can begin. I urge you to think of all kinds of ways to face *ar* and repeat it out loud often. Is there anything in the room he can think of that has the *ar* sound? Have him make a card of the word and tape it to the object. When you are in the yard, remind your student he is standing on *ar*, y*ar*d. When he gets in the *car*, what pattern can he spell? At night when the st*ars* are out, point to the sky. Is there any *ar* pattern to think about?

The students who in the past have had difficulty with the following words could include them for review at this time because the *ar* sound can be heard: *ear, hear, fear, rear, dear, near, soar, roar*.

If your student's hand coordination is good, have him look at the words in the story and underline the *ar* pattern. If he cannot draw the line accurately, ask him to point his pencil to the pattern while you underline the *ar*. This procedure is an extra exercise that should in future lessons be encouraged when meeting each new phonic integral.

NOTE on *end* pattern: Help your student decode the words with *end* by giving him the *en* sound, then he can use the Seven Special Steps: *bend, send, mend, then.*

WORD LIST

bar	cart	bark	hard
car	dart	dark	card
far	start	lark	lard
jar	chart	mark	yard
tar		park	farm
star		Clark	large
scar		shark	
		stark	

SILLY STORY

Carl and His Car

At the end of the bend in the road, Carl drove his car up beside the trees. Carl started to slide from his car to see the dark mark the farm cart made. The farm cart had made a scar on Carl's white car when the farm cart drove by.

All at once Carl could hear a wild bark. A large dog in the yard came barking at Carl's white car. Carl did not like the wild voice of the dog. Carl had no choice. He could see that he should slide into the car. Carl did dart into his car. He made the car start. Then he drove home to his barn on his farm where his nice dog greeted him, but his dog did not bark. Carl said he did feel fine to be at home on his farm.

Carl did not care any more if his white car had a scar on the side. He would send his car to town. The man in town would mend his car.

Feed Words: without, any, town, dog.

LESSON 53

Phonics: The *all, ing* pattern

In the next two lessons, you will teach first the *all* family of words, then the *ing* family. At the first lesson have the student print *all*. Ask him what letter he can put before *all* to make another word. Help him guess through the list. Have him print each word. Follow the same plan for the *ing* family of words.

In the Silly Story the words *signs, explain,* and *buy* can be analyzed. Cover the *ex* with the card. Have the child analyze the word *plain.* Give your student the sound of *ex.*

Show your student that the word *buy* is like the word *by.* Two different meanings, two different spellings, but one sound! No wonder Frenchmen think English is hard to learn!

Give your student the sound of *wh* as in the word *while.* This is a digraph, *not* a blend. (The *wh* has another sound in the word *who.* Do not make the comparison at this time.)

Spelling words: while, whale, white.

WORD LISTS

all	fall	tall	ring	sling
ball	hall	wall	sing	cling
call	mall	stall	swing	bring
			spring	fling
			sting	king
			ding-a-ling	

SILLY STORIES

In the Mall

All the stores in the mall face a tall wall. On the wall is a sign to explain all you should buy in the stores.

You should find all kinds of prizes to buy in the mall. You can buy the prizes if you have money!

NOTE: See if your child can guess the last word.

The King on a Swing

In the spring the king likes to swing from the tall tree in his kingdom.

A lady in the kingdom gave the king a nice rope. The king used the rope to make a swing.

The lady likes to see the king cling to the swing while he sings in the breeze.

Feed Word: from.

LESSON 54

Phonics: Adding *er, ed, ing*

The suffix *ed* usually has the sound of *t* when added to a word, or it can have the sound *ed* or *id*. Because *d* is the last consonant and because the child is familiar with the *d* sound, you can suggest the sound will be *d*. The student uses these words with the *ed* suffix in conversation so often he soon learns to select the correct sound once he has made the analyzing process automatic.

Read the following sentences to your student. Ask him if each sentence means the same thing.

> I am a jumper.
> I am jumping.
> Yesterday I jumped.

Do not try to explain that the verb *jump* can change its tense as well as turn into a noun. Explain only that with some words you can add special extra letters that will change the word. Just like when you put white paint into red you get pink. Or you can add blue paint to red and you get purple. We can make our words paint new pictures with just a little change.

Now tell your student that some of the words he has learned can change by adding *er, ed,* or *ing*. We first have to do something special to the words that end in *e*.

On a piece of paper print the word *bake*. Cross out the *e*. Print *bak* three times. Add *er, ed, ing*. Have your student read the words you have printed.

At the top of a paper print *er, ed, ing*. Then print in a column the words *race, dice, ride, nice*. Ask your student how he can add the ending *er* to these words. He will promptly forget you crossed out the *e*. He will probably add *er* without crossing out the *e* and erasing it. Just correct him gently by saying, "Do you remember we have to cross something out?" Have your student (1) cross out the letter *e*, (2) erase it, and (3) add *er*.

Have the child take the same three steps with the *ed* ending, then the *ing* ending.

The next day on this lesson give the child these new words to use for the new endings: *make, time, hate, use, hike, eat*.

For the student's reading lesson have him read the words with the new endings.

SILLY STORIES

A Sailing Day

Dave is sailing on the sea today. Dave is not bailing the boat. The boat is not leaking.

Dave is leaning on the side of the boat. The sail is sweeping into the breeze.

Sailing in the breeze is a fine feeling. Would you like to be sailing on the sea?

Poking, Biting or Fighting

At times I feel like poking, biting, and fighting. I hope I would see that poking, biting, and fighting would be mean. I would not care to have Jean or Jake or Jane poke, bite, or fight me.

LESSON 55

Extra Words

The words *or* and *from* have been used as Feed Words. Now you can compare *on* and *or*. They both start with the same sound. Your student can decode *or*.

Repeat the consonant blend sound of *fr*. Can your pupil print the letter combination of this sound? (If he cannot, stop right here and review the consonant blend sounds with *r*. You may need to go back to some of the lessons for review. Do not show irritation if your student is making errors. Just tell him we all have to review information that is new to us.) When your student has success in printing *fr* after *hearing* you repeat it, have him then print the word *on* (spell it for him). Now can he spell and print the sound of *om*? Combine on paper *fr* and *om*. Ask your pupil to read the word *from* which can be placed in the short *o* envelope.

This procedure seems lengthy but it is most important. The word *from* is misread by many students, especially the dyslexics, if they have not been thoroughly exposed to the components. The misreading can be *form*, *for*, or *foam*, thus completely garbling the meaning of the sentence.

When your student is looking for something to do on a rainy day, ask him to set up an office for special work. If there is no desk or table available to him, can you find some big cardboard cartons to make an office desk? Then give your student an old newspaper or magazine. He can cut out articles and underline with his red pen the consonant blend where *r* or *l* is the second letter (*bl, br,* etc.).

LESSON 56

Phonics: The *ou, ow* pattern

Explain to your student that he is going to learn one of the sounds that *ou* and *ow* makes is *owwww*, just like the sound he makes if someone pokes him too hard. (Much later he will find that in some words *ou* and *ow* have the long *o* sound — *four, blow.*)

In the Silly Stories keep asking, "What sound do *ou* and *ow* make?"

Have your child underline words in magazines with *ou* and *ow*. The student does not have to analyze these words unless he wants to. The exercise is to stimulate the child to focus on a specific pattern (visual sorting).

REMINDER: Some words that your child does not use in his conversation are included in the Silly Stories. Talk about these words. *Stout* will be a new word. You can explain that the word *fat* is used more often. What are some other words he knows that might make the picture of something fat in his mind? (*huge, big, large,* etc.) It is important to show your student that words are like paint. A blue sky suggests a nice day, a dark blue-gray sky suggests a storm. Words, like paint, can suggest different pictures. Some words paint only slight differences — *stout, fat, big.*

Notice that the words *could, would* and *should* have the *ou* pattern. Your student learned these as an *ould* pattern. He probably will not notice the *ou*. However, if he does discover the *ou* in these three words, praise your pupil for his keenness. Then you can explain that sometimes *ou* has a different sound. Right now he is going to learn those words that belong to the *ou* sound as in the word *stout.*

Your student can decode the word m<u>an</u> if you underline *an*.

WORD LIST

cow	cow		
dow	down		
fow	fowl		
gow	gown		
how	how	howl	
now	now		
tow	town		
clow	clown		
crow	crown	crowd	
brow	brow	brown	
frow	frown		
grow	growl		

ou	our	out
bou	bound	
cou	count	
fou	foul	
hou	house	
lou	loud	
pou	pout	
mou	mound	
sou	sour	
sou	south	
blou	blouse	
clou	cloud	
flou	flour	
grou	ground	
prou	proud	
scou	scour	
spou	spout	
stou	stout	
shou	shout	

→

SILLY STORIES

The Owl Howled

The owl howled a loud sound. The clown found he became scared by the loud howl. The clown could not find out if the owl howled from the tree or from the ground.

The clown said he would shout a loud sound. Maybe the loud shout would scare the proud owl.

Twice the clown shouted a loud sound. The proud owl howled his loud sound. Then a crowd drove down the street from the town. The crowd drove to the trees to find where all the loud sounds came from. The crowd came to the place where they could hear the clown shouting loud sounds.

"Clown, why do you shout?" cried a stout man.

"Man," said the clown, "I am trying to scare the owl. At night the howls of the owl scare me and my cow. My cow can not give milk when the howling owl scares her.

"Now I am trying to scare the loud owl. I would like the owl to go away. My cow and I would feel fine if the owl would take his loud howls away from my house."

Feed Words: why, where, said.   →

A Mouse, A Mouse

"A mouse, a mouse," shouted Joyce.

"Where is the mouse, Joyce?" asked Howard.

"It is crouching under the couch, Howard."

"Oh! Now I see the mouse under the couch. Shh, shh. We cannot make a sound, Joyce. I am a Boy Scout and you are a Girl Scout. We can rout the mouse out."

Howard and Joyce chased the mouse round and round the house.

Howard said, "Joyce, you are a brave mouse scout."

"Howard, you are a brave mouse scout," said Joyce. "We can be proud we are fine mouse scouts."

Feed Words: where, under, said, asked.

LESSON 57

Phonics: Digraph *ch*

Your student has met the digraphs *th, sh,* and *wh.*
Do not let him confuse these consonant forms with
the consonant blends. Ask him if he can name some
consonant blends. If he is having trouble, give him
the clue *bl, br, cl.* Point out to him that he can still
hear each letter in these blends, whereas he cannot
hear the individual letter sounds in these patterns:
th, wh, and *ch.* These combinations have special
sounds that seem to come from out of nowhere.
Many students think that any two consonants together form blends. To avoid this mistake, I have
tried to acquaint the student with the special blend
pattern of *bl, br, cl, cr,* and point out that the
digraph pattern has *h* present, as in *ch, sh, th, wh.*
Later your student will find out that there are
other consonant blends and digraphs that will not
fit these patterns. However, you do not want to
overload the student with exceptions at this time.

Phonics: z

Your student is ready for the letter *z.* Teach the
capital Z first. Then explain that the small *z* is the
same thing only he is to make it smaller in the
bottom part of the lined box. The letter *z* starts like
capital *T.* A straight line across the top. At the end
of this line, point back to the bottom corner. Then
draw a line across the bottom.

The sound of *z* starts like the *s* sound but continues
with a buzzing sound that tickles the tongue.

WORD LIST

coach   beach
poach   leech
roach   peach
             teach
             bleach
             screech
             speech

cheek   choke   chide   chain
cheer   chore   chime   chair
cheese   chose   child   chase
cheat

SILLY STORY

Greedy Mr. Goat

Mr. Goat liked to eat cheese. He would fill his cheeks with the cheese. If he could find a peach he would fill his cheeks with the peach.

Mrs. Toad would hide behind the chair. She would see Mr. Goat take a bite of cheese. He would take a bite of peach.

Then one day Mrs. Toad peeked from behind the chair. She could see Mr. Goat going to reach for the cheese. He could not see the roach that was on the cheese. Mr. Goat was going to take a greedy bite. Mrs. Toad gave a huge screech.

Mr. Goat became so scared he bolted from the home. Mrs. Toad had saved Mr. Goat from choking. He did not eat the mean roach. Mrs. Toad seemed so wise to teach Mr. Goat not to be so greedy.

→

WORD LIST

haze*	gaze	doze
breeze	freeze	froze

SILLY POEM

Z

I gaze

In the haze.

I doze

In the breeze.

I can't freeze

If the breeze

Is warm.

Feed Words: can't, warm.

---

* You will need to explain the meaning of some of these words.

LESSON 58

Phonics: The one sound of er, ir, ur, wor

Your pupil has been exposed to the sound of *er*. You can tell him that for some strange reason the sound of *er* can be written several ways. Right now he knows *er*. He can combine stick friend *i* with *r*, getting *ir*. Then there is *ur*, with the letter *u* really being two sticks hitched at the bottom. Demonstrate this. Have your student print these forms (and type). You can also tell him that his new friendly word *or* changes its sound when *w* sits in front, *work*. The letter *w* has much power, it can make the next vowel in front of it change its normal sound. (Soon there is a lesson on *wa, warn*.)

The student with a poor visual memory has to keep working with these words for spelling because it is so difficult for him to remember which word has what combination. This lesson can be divided into two parts. You can judge how much should be covered at a time. Remember, most students should read each story a minimum of three separate times if reading is difficult for them.

For most students you will have to talk about the patterns of each word before they start to print. Also, be sure to have your student place lines under the new phonics patterns he is studying where they appear in the words of the Silly Story.

NOTE: Your student knows the word *at*. Can he decode *cat*?

Sentences for dictation (four separate days): When you dictate a word, a student often has trouble forming a mental picture of the word you are speaking. You must help him try to analyze the sounds and associate the letter patterns with the sounds. For each set of sentences announce what vowel pattern you will be stressing in some of the words. He will not be able to decide between *er*, *ir*, or *ur* yet. You have to help him in this memory work.

1. Her fern is nice.
2. The herd of cows is huge.
3. The clerk is in the store.

1. I can hear the bird chirp.
2. The girl has a brown skirt.
3. Craig has a brown shirt.

1. The burn hurt Kurt.
2. She has a nice curl in her hair.
3. The nurse has a brown purse.

WORD LIST

er	her	jerk	herd	term	fern	clerk
	were					
er	neater	leaner	leader	reader	beater	heater
	eater	floater	loader			
ur	fur	burn	turn	hurt	curb	purr
	curl	hurl	nurse	purse		
ir	sir	fir	bird	girl	dirt	first
	thirst	shirt	skirt	birth	third	chirp
wor	word	work	worth	world	worse	worm
	worst					

SILLY SENTENCES

1. My work is hard.
2. The worm is brown.
3. The world is huge.

→

SILLY STORIES

The Cat on the Curb

One day I did see a cat on the curb. He seemed to be curled up like a curve. First a girl came by. She did not say a word. She liked to hear the cat purr. That cat did not stir. He stayed asleep on the dirt. Even though he did sleep, you could hear that cat purr.

All at once a bird in the tree nearby gave a chirp. The chirp seemed loud. Then an owl made the worst sound. I gave a shout from my mouth. The girl made a growling sound.

The cat began to stir. Then he gave a jerk and raced into the house. All that noise seemed too loud for the kitty cat.

Feed Words: why, even, once, kitty, cat.

Bertha's Birthday

The girl who moved from the South had a birthday today. This girl from the South is named Bertha.

Her friends Fern and Irma made a cake for Bertha. They almost burned the cake. However, Fern turned off the stove and saved the cake.

Bertha, Fern and Irma were thirsty so they made grape juice. Making the cake seemed like more work than making grape juice. Really the girls did not mind the work. It seemed nice to surprise Bertha on her birthday.

Feed Words: who, off, friends.

177

LESSON 59

Phonics: The wa pattern

When your student meets *w*, he must put on his brakes so that he can find what strange thing *w* has done to the vowel. He must ask, "Do I see a peanut butter and jelly word or a layer-cake pattern?": *wait, waist, waste, way, wake, wave, wage, wade, wore.*

If the word does not have either of these patterns, then he must ask himself, "Do I see *or* hitched to *w*?" (the *er* sound). If he does not find *wor*, he may find *wa* and the sound will be the *wa* as in *wall*. He makes the regular *w* sound and adds the *a* (which really has the sound of short *u* but do not confuse your pupil with this information).

Some teachers tell the student to find small words in the big ones. This exercise works in words like *grant* but will not be valid for words like *want*. The emphasis should be placed on the patterns he is building, not the small words. Focusing on *wa* helps the pupil with that word *want*, which is so often misread as *went*, and with another word that is so troublesome for the dyslexic, the word *was*. Do you realize that the words *was* and *saw*, which are reversible, have not been used up to this point in the Integral Phonics Reading Program? The pupil is trained to sift out the *wa* as a starting point; the *s* becomes secondary. This word *was* will be used many many times before the student faces the word *saw*, when *au, aw* patterns are introduced as the last phonics integral in this book.

Even with this extreme care in the training of the eye and brain pathways, a dyslexic student may be trapped into reversals. However, he can recognize what he has done wrong and make the correction, whereas the student who has been introduced to *was* and *saw* and other reversibles as sight words constantly remains in confusion.

When your student meets the word *war*, he may focus on the *ar* pattern. Remind him, "Beware of the letter *w* at the beginning of a word." Even if the pupil does pick up the *ar* pattern in *war*, he soon makes the sound adjustment.

When your student faces words with short *a* intensively, he will meet *wag, wax,* and *wagon*, where the sound is not like *war*. These words, however, fit into another category, which will eliminate trouble.

WORD LIST

war	wart	water
ward	was	want
warm	wasp	wall
warn	wash	waltz
warp	watch	walk*

* silent *l*

LESSON 60

Extra words: Consonant digraphs

You have already given your student the sound of *wh*. Review these words: *while, whale, white*. Can your student print the *th* sound? Remind him that he now has had *th, wh, sh, ch*, and silent *gh*. These are consonant digraphs (two letters that separately have specific sounds but do not carry these sounds when they join together).

Play The Game with these words: *the, they, that, than* (add th*is*), *shake, shame, shade, shy, shine, shore, sheet, shout;* the *ight* list; and the *ch* list; as well as *white, while, whale, then, when*. Before you start, put the last two words in front of your student. Can he decode them? Are you giving enough praise?

Phonics: *oo, ew*

Explain to your student that the next set of vowel patterns can have several sounds. Again he will not have to worry about all the variations. Can he pucker his lips up like a pig's snout? (It is fun to have a mirror for the child to see his lips.) Now can he say the sound *oooooo* (as in *boot*)? The sound comes out of the round hole his lips make and he will print (and type) round circles for *oo, oo, oo*. Can he print *boot*? Can he print any other words with this sound?

Have the student decode the Word List. Somehow we English-speaking people do not like to leave these two holes (*oo*) at the end of a word. Most of the time when we have the *oo* sound at the end of a sentence we change the letters entirely. We at least choose the round-shaped letter of *e* but then we finish with a *w*. Can he decode the *ew* list, then read the story? Some students will need to read the first Silly Story three to five times before the *oo* pattern registers (it does not have to be perfect). Other students will be able to move quickly to the *My Stew* story.

SILLY STORIES

The Moose and the Goose

One day a moose and a goose went for a walk down the dirt road. All at once the goose gave a whoop and a hoot. Goose told Moose to boost him into the tree. Moose scooped Goose up into the tree.

Moose said, "Goose, why do you feel you should be in the tree?"

Goose said, "I was sure I could feel Slew, the shrew, under the ground. I am afraid Slew, the shrew, will poke his nose out of his groove and chew my feet as I walk down the dirt road."

Moose said, "Goose, you have no proof that Slew, the shrew, is creeping in a groove under this road. I will stoop down to try to hear if Slew, the shrew, is trying to chew his way up to our feet."

Soon a huge boom sounded in the air. Goose flew as fast as he could fly and Moose did scoot down the dirt road.

Moose and Goose never did find out if Slew, the shrew, really was in his groove under the dirt road.

Feed Words: under, fast, never, once, up, you.

My Stew

In one of the rooms in my house I like to sit on a stool and eat stew.

One night when the moon was bright a goose flew on to the roof of our house. He could see that I was eating my stew with my spoon from my plate.

The goose flew down from the roof. He flew into the room of my house, where I was eating my stew. He made a loud hoot and a toot. He tried to say he would like my stew.

I threw a pile of beans to the goose. He would not eat the beans. I threw a pile of peas to the goose. He would not eat the peas.

At last I put down a plate of stew. That made the goose hoot and toot with joy.

FOUR:
SHORT VOWELS

What phonic structures are used in the following section?

This section is composed of lessons on the short vowels. Your student has gradually been exposed to these sounds throughout the previous two sections. You will continue your instruction using the same format that is familiar to you. The Seven Special Steps are used when meeting these short, small sandwich words that have only one-vowel filling. Tell your student that the short-vowel words are too skimpy to allow for a second silent vowel.

These short vowels do not use the sounds of their alphabet names. Associating a second sound for these letters is difficult. Your student, however, can give full attention to this new task because he has already mastered the basic decoding procedure.

In school, the teacher probably uses pictures to help the child identify the sounds. If you feel this will help, cut out an apple picture and write *a* for apple under the picture. Put *e* under the egg picture, *i* under an Indian, and *u* under an umbrella. In the Integral Phonics Reading Program, the short vowels are dramatized by unpleasant sounds that the child laughs about. Any new inspiration you develop that helps the student remember will be valid.

What do I do if my student is still having trouble with some of the phonic integrals?

If your student has trouble with a particular phonic integral, review a lesson that features that unit. When you notice confusion with one specific item, have the student listen to the sound, repeat it, then he should print a few of the words that use that integral.

As the student grows, he will be able to handle quite complex comparisons and contrasts, such as words like *fist* and *first, form* and *from,* etc. Lessons with words that have both long *i* and short *i* in sentences are given when the student has had sufficient experience with each integral. The other vowel combinations will be programmed in a similar manner.

In many phonics programs, some of the phonic integrals that are not introduced in *The Natural Way to Reading* are thrown right into the beginning readers' lessons, causing many students to become hopelessly muddled. If you find that your student still needs carefully planned extra work, I would recommend that you continue with the IPRP. Other students may be strong enough to begin to use any of the alternative programs offered in the classroom.

Why do many students have difficulty with spelling?

Many people assume that if the student can see and read a word, the sequence of the letters should be so obvious that when that person wants to print the word, he can, if he tries hard enough, recall the correct spelling. Written spelling work is so intricate that even those with highly efficient nervous systems find their success less than adequate.

After the teacher gives oral dictation, the student

182

must first register the word with enough comprehension that its meaning will flash a picture of the concept. Dr. Norman Geschwind tells us that when a person wishes to write that word, the auditory pattern that registers on the angular gyrus must produce a visual pattern of that sound.[1] To do this, the student in the beginning stages literally mouths the word. He then has to register each phoneme (the letter sound), which must be changed into a grapheme (a printed shape of the letter sound) and hold this in his mind long enough to allow for the processing necessary to transfer that phoneme-grapheme into finger-pencil action. This entire description is grossly oversimplified but it does convey the complications of spelling.

You notice that I have used the shorthand words *phoneme* and *grapheme*, which I would not have burdened you with at the beginning of the book while you were probably struggling with enough rusty terms. If too much new material had been presented too soon, you would have abandoned the book. Your student, also, cannot be overwhelmed by too many demands while learning to spell.

Now that my student can decode, has he at last completed the neurological steps necessary to be a successful reader?

You have just taken your child over the first mountain in the range of neurological steps to be scaled. During this time you have been a key figure in your child's progress. You have taught your student decoding, one of the tasks in the reading process that involves the nervous system. Do you remember when your child was learning to walk, you gave him plenty of time, space, and encouragement, without deadlines to meet? At that point you did not have to be a skilled teacher of walking to help him. In fact, if he was blessed with health, he walked in spite of you not because of you.

In this latest developmental process, unlike his earlier neurological growth stages, your student has been completely dependent upon your skill in following the directions of a book, and you have had to insist upon deadlines as well. Your child has been able to take this mammoth leap forward because you made the effort to help him. He will continue to grow into a productive reader.

In the past, very few educators, unfortunately, have been fully aware of the demands schooling places on the nervous system of the individual. The work of Samuel Torrey Orton, M.D., and those pioneers who have realized the neurological im-plications that learning entails have only recently come to the attention of the pedagogist.

At this time, you can take pride in the fact that by teaching decoding skill, you have brought your student through one of the most important facets in his neurological growth.

If you would like to study more about the technical aspects of this developmental process, you may want to join the Orton Society, a scientific and educational organization named after the neurologist who did so much to alert concerned people of various disciplines. Membership entitles you to reading material, reading lists, and other services. The address is: Suite 206, 8415 Bellona Lane, Towson, Maryland 21204. The state and national associations of specific learning disabilities also have much to offer.

[1] Norman Geschwind, "Language and the Brain," *Scientific American* (April, 1972), p. 79.

LESSON 61

Phonics: Short a

Your student has already been using short *a*. We are going to call attention to it for more extensive use. You can explain that in the Word Lists he has been reading the vowels are the long ones that say their names. What are these vowels? Do not be upset if after all this time he cannot list the vowels. In the future you may need to keep asking him the list of these letters.

Your student realizes that some consonants have more than one sound. Now we are going to give a new sound to each of the vowels. These are called short sounds.

Print for reading the words *at, as, am, an, and*. Whether he remembers these or not, you can explain to your pupil that you will concentrate on the sound of that *a*. The short vowels he is going to study make very short words. They are sandwich words with only *one* filling. The first group of words will have a very thick slice of bread on one side. Big tall *k* is very lonely with just one short vowel so he asks silent *c* to stand beside him. (Open-shaped *c* is going to sit beside closed circle ɑ, who leans on a stick.)

I suggest that short *a* has a disagreeable sound. When your student dislikes some mess he sees he says *ack*. (Accentuate the sound by making a facial expression of distaste. Repeat dramatically that sound several times.) Have your student repeat the sound, holding onto it. Now he can decode the Word List. Have him write (and type) a few of the words you dictate to him. Be sure that he makes a conscious effort to listen to and then repeat each sound part of the word. (By doing this in each lesson you are giving your student invaluable training, which helps him to strengthen the neurological pathways that have a different sequencing from the pathways used for reading.)

Now your student can read his new story. Be sure to use the Seven Special Steps. (If he is having troubles with a new vowel integral, point to the vowel, then have him repeat the sound and *drag* it out. Then you repeat that vowel sound, holding onto it out loud while you point to that first consonant that directs your pupil to blend the consonant to that vowel sound.)

Your student will meet the word *knew* in this lesson. He knows that we have words that sometimes have silent letters in them. Explain that the letter *n* sometimes likes to put silent *k* in front of it. Can he decode *knew, knife, knee*?

Sentences for dictation to be used when working with short vowels:

1. The cat sat on the back of the cab.
2. Frank can tramp to the camp.
3. Nan and Pam had a fat snack.

1. Bill will sit still.
2. Jill can sit on the hill.
3. Dick will slip on the ice.

1. Bob would not hit the frog.
2. That dog is cross.
3. I will drop a rock on the dock.

1. Russ stuck the nut in the tub.
2. I must trust the duck.
3. She must clean the dust off the tub.

1. Nell went to the tent.
2. Chet sent a pen to Bess.
3. I will mend the vest.

WORD LIST

back	sack	rack	track
pack	hack	black	stack
tack	Jack	crack	snack
lack	Mack	slack	smack

SILLY STORY

Mack, the Huge Black Mule

Mack, the huge black mule, drove the cart smack into a wall. The pack on the black mule's back flew down to the ground.

Jack was in the cart. He was trying to keep Mack, the huge black mule, on the wide tracks in the dirt road.

Mack was feeling mean. He refused to drive the cart in the wide tracks.

Mack, the huge black mule, knew the pack on his back had candy in it. He knew it would be nice to have a few bites of candy. Mack knew that his driver named Jack would not feed his huge black mule the candy.

Mack decided he would be mean. He would drive smack into the wall. The sack of candy would fall out of the pack. Then Mack could get at the candy on the ground.

Before Jack, the driver, could get the candy back in the sack, Mack, the mule, had eaten most of that candy.

LESSON 62

Extra Words

You can help your student reorganize his envelopes. The words on cards for the Extra Words envelope are those listed in the previous lesson. You may feel that, at this time, the envelopes can be discarded. You should keep making new cards from each Word List for The Game.

Phonics: *an, am* patterns

The Word List in this lesson makes the student decide between the last letter sound of *n* or *m*. When dictating the words, remind your pupil that the letter *m* has three humps. He cannot make the sound of *m* without lifting his lips. His lips have to hump over the sound. If he has to, he can say the letter *n* without shaping his lips at all. The tongue does the work.

Your student can read *Nan's Plan*, a story that gives review in many areas.

WORD LIST

ham	Sam	dam	clam
Pam	scram	slam	can
pan	ran	tan	van

jam	ram	tam	lamb
Dan	fan	man	Nan
ban	bran	plan	than

SILLY STORY

Nan's Plan

Nan had a plan. Nan said she would soon decide if she would invite Pam to share her plan.

Nan decided to have Pam work with her. Pam was pleased that Nan invited her to share the plan.

Nan told Pam she would arise at five in the morning. She would drive her bike to Dan's house. You see, this day would be Dan's birthday.

Nan told Pam she had an alarm clock that she would put in a big can. Nan planned to set the alarm for five thirty. Nan's plan was to put the can with the alarm clock under Dan's window beside his house.

The day arrived that was Dan's birthday. Nan and Pam rode on their bikes to Dan's house. They put the can under Dan's window. Then the girls went to hide behind the barn.

All at once the alarm gave its loud sound. Brrrrring, brrrrrring! Dan appeared at the window. Then he raced down to the can with the clock. He turned off the alarm. Then he found a note in the can.

Nan and Pam were peeking around the barn. They could see that Dan was reading the note.

It was Nan who wrote the note. The note told Dan to go up the hill in back of the barn. There he would find a surprise. Dan ran up the hill. What did he see tied to the tree?

A tiny black lamb with a note tied to the rope, was what Dan saw.

It said, "Happy Birthday to Dan."

From,
Nan and Pam

Feed Words: under, who, what.

LESSON 63

Extra Words

Review the Extra Words *would, could, should, to, too, do, mother, said, put.*

Add three new words: *here, there, where.* Explain that each one of these words points out something. The book is *here.* The book is *there.* *Where* is the book? Show your pupil that *here* is in the words *there* and *where.* The word *here* has the long *e* sound, but even though the last three letters of each word are the same, the first *e* changes to the sound more like long *a.*

Phonics: *ad, ab* patterns

In this lesson the student will need to read accurately the words with *d* and *b.* If your student has been trained to form the letter *d* by starting with *o* and the letter *b* by starting like *h,* he will not have difficulty with these mirror-image letters. If the dyslexic student is still reversing these letters, be sure to have him write the words to dictation *before* he reads the list. You will soon see what difficulties he faces.

When he confuses the directional shape of *d,* ask him whether he feels the *d* sound on his lips or in his throat. The feeling is, of course, in the round circle in his throat, just as round as the starting circle of the letter *d.* The letter *b* starts with that tall stick line (the mast on the *b*oat).

After your student prints some of the words from the list, he can decode the story *The Mad Crab.* Are you having the phonic pattern underlined in the stories?

WORD LIST

bad	lad	cab	grab
cad	mad	dab	crab
Dad	pad	jab	slab
fad	sad	nab	stab
had	glad	blab	drab

SILLY STORY

The Mad Crab

Once there was a mad crab who enjoyed sneaking around the sand by the sea. One day a lad named Brad was sleeping on a thin pad on the beach.

All at once Brad could feel a bad stab under the pad. He gave a jab and a poke in the pad where the bad crab had poked him.

Brad was in for a big surprise. The surprise did not make Brad very glad. That mad crab gave a stab and chewed the end of Brad's finger.

Feed Words: very, once, under, end.

LESSON 64

Extra Words

Add the word *very*. Explain that *y* at the end of a word can change its sound to *i*. It sometimes takes on the sound of *e*. Ask for the sound of *er, ir, ur*. (Do not be disappointed with a wrong answer. Joke about the trick the brain is playing. That *er* may be stuck in some corner.) Then you have to explain that *v* changes the *er* sound. Can he unscramble the word to get the correct pronunciation of *very*?

Phonics: Short *i*

By this time the student can read the word *in*. You can tell him this word is the first sound in *In*dian. That first vowel sound is short *i*. Another way to remind your student of the sound of short *i* is first to review the short *a* sound. He says *ack* when he dislikes something. When he is *sick* he may say he has an *icky* feeling. Every so often, review these vowel sounds. (You will have to help him *many, many* times before the information is solidly imprinted for recall.)

Now have your pupil print *in*, then he can try: *pin, fin, sin, skin*. Can he add the extra *k* for *sink, pink, mink?*

By printing the spelling words before he reads, the student anchors the vowel pattern through sensory expression. There seems to be an added advantage to getting the fingers to carry out the orders of the brain. Hopefully, a conscious effort has been made when the pupil receives the sound from outside and processes it to the final point of pencil to paper. (The typing experience adds one more reinforcement.) Have the student read the Word List for the Silly Sentences. Another day the story can be read.

Sentences for dictation:

1. Bill will not prick his skin with a pin. (Explain that the word *with* has a short *i*. Pronounce *wi*. Have the student print *wi*, then pronounce *th* for him to translate into printing.)
2. I think I will *wash* the sink.
3. The twin boys are named Dick and Nick.

4. Jack and Jill sit on a hill. (For some silly reason, short *i* with *l* (*il*) wants an extra *l*.)

The next lesson has sentences for dictation, the Word List, and two Silly Stories for reading. Follow the usual lesson plan.

LESSON 65

Phonics: Short *i* (continued)

WORD LIST

Dick	grip	twin	rib
Nick	lip	fin	bib
kick	dip	pin	crib
lick	rip	skin	fib
pick	sip	sin	
quick	slip	bin	wrist
sick	ship	win	fist
tick			his
wick	Jill	twig	sister
click	Bill	big	
flick	will	fig	
prick	still	rig	
stick	fill		
slick	hill	think	
trick	pill	sink	
brick	grill	kink	
	drill	pink	
	mill	mink	

→

SILLY SENTENCES

1. Bill and Mack will pick the black crab to eat.
2. Will the cat lick the plate?
3. Jill can fill the big pail with wat<u>er</u>.
4. My sist<u>er</u> will play kick the can.
5. Do not slip on the ice.
6. Mack will not fight with his fist.
7. Bill will not prick his skin with a pin.
8. I think I will wash the sink.
9. The twin boys are named Dick and Nick.
10. Jack and Jill sit on the hill.

NOTE: Your student has already printed the following sentences. Notice that he has to decode as if he had never seen them.

SILLY STORY

Trink, the Mink

There was a little mink name<u>d</u> Trink. He was a frisky little mink. He could not keep still. He like<u>d</u> to skip and slip and slink around all over the place.

Mother Mink told Trink, the mink, he would have to take time to sit still. Trink, the mink, did try to sit still but soon he decide<u>d</u> he neede<u>d</u> a drink of water.

Trink, the mink, made a fast dash to the pool to get a drink. He dash<u>ed</u> so fast he gave a skid and what do you think happen<u>ed</u>? Trink, the mink, spill<u>ed</u> right into the pool.

Trink, the mink, did not care. He had a drink and a swim, too.

LESSON 66

Phonics: Short *i* with short *a* review

SILLY STORY

The Mule in the Sink

Nick had a sick mule named Clinker. Nick decided Clinker might not be sick if he gave his mule a bath.

No one was at home at Nick's farm house. So Nick marched Clinker, the mule, into his kitchen.

Nick decided he would try to put Clinker into the big farm house sink. Nick put a long plank of wood on the floor and slanted it up to the sink.

Nick wanted Clinker to march up the plank and stand in the big sink. Now you can imagine what Clinker was thinking. You are right. Clinker was thinking that Nick could not be too bright. After all, why should Clinker have to stand in a kitchen sink to have a bath. A bath would not cure Clinker, the mule.

Clinker clicked his back heels first. Then he flicked his front legs into the air. Nick became very scared. Nick grabbed Clinker's rope and dashed his mule out of the kitchen as fast as he could.

Nick realized he would have to find a different cure for Clinker.

LESSON 67

Phonics: Short *o*

Ask if your student remembers the sound of short *i*. Then repeat for him the words *tick-tock*. The word *tick* has what kind of a vowel in it? Now your pupil is going to study the vowel sound in the word *tock*, the short *o*. It also is the sound that an *orange* starts with. Can the student read the short *o* Word List?

Point out to your student that in little words, short *i* followed by *l* wants an extra *l*. The letter *i* is a short straight stick. The letter *l* is a tall stick. Now there are three sticks in a row as in *fill*. Short *o* demands that when *s* is the last letter after *o* it wants a second *s*. Circle *o* wants two of that winding *s*, as in *toss*.

The student can read the Silly Stories and during a later lesson he can read the Silly Sentences that have both short *o* and long *o* words. Remind your pupil to see if *e* frosting is at the end of a layer-cake word. What hint does that give him about the sound of that first vowel? (This is review that may be very rusty. Be friendly and reteach if necessary. Just do not show impatience.)

Follow the usual directions for the lesson after this. Are you using the Word Lists to play The Game?

WORD LIST

Bob	cod	bog	rock	top
cob	nod	hog	lock	hop
job	pod	cog	dock	mop
mob		dog	sock	stop
rob		log	stock	slop
slob		frog	hockey	flop
blob		flog	jockey	shop
		jog	rocker	chop
			locker	flop
				crop
				drop

loss	lot	doll	pond	other
moss	rot	Molly	blond	another
toss	hot			
gloss	dot	long	box	
cross	not	ding-dong		
floss	pot			
	blot			
	cot			
	clot			
	trot			
	spot			
	shot			

→

SILLY SENTENCES

1. Can you see Cape Cod on the map?
2. Bob and Tom grew a crop of hay.
3. The frog will flop in the water.
4. Tom's dog can jog along the road.
5. Bob will toss a bone to his dog.
6. Tom will poke the log across the pond.
7. I can lock the top of the box.
8. We hope that spot is free of slime.
9. You can drop the rock onto the dock.
10. The lot has moss on it.
11. He can mop the top of the dock.
12. Tom could toss the rope to the dog.

SILLY STORY

The Big Fat Frog

The big fat frog looks like a slob as he jogs along the swamp. At times when he sits on a log he looks like a blob of wood.

A cross boy threw a rock near the moss where the frog had stopped on the log. The frog gave a hop and flopped into the water. He gave a huge splash that made the cross boy get sopping wet. Now he was really angry at the big fat frog. He threw another rock at the frog. Along came a dog who saw the cross boy toss the rock at the big fat frog.

The dog began to snarl at the cross boy. By this time the cross boy did not dare to toss the other rock in his hand. He let the rock drop from his hand.

The dog continued to snarl and bark. The cross boy gave up. He ran home. The big fat frog was grateful to the nice dog.

Feed Words: who, grateful.

LESSON 68

Phonics: Short *o* (continued)

SILLY STORY

Bob and Molly

Bob had a sister named Molly. Bob liked to tease Molly. He had a tiny frog he called Dot. Bob would try to scare Molly by putting the tiny frog near her.

Bob was sure Molly would be scared by the tiny frog. However, Molly gave Bob a surprise. Molly liked to tease Bob as much as Bob liked to tease Molly.

Molly went to the swamp and captured a big fat frog. Molly put the big fat frog in a box. When Molly got home she named her frog Slob.

When Bob was asleep in bed Molly sneaked into Bob's room. She put Slob, the frog, in Bob's room. She put Slob, the frog, on Bob's bed.

Molly did not realize that Bob had put his tiny frog named Dot under Molly's bed.

Just as Molly was about to fall asleep, Dot, the frog, leaped on her bed. At the same time Slob, the frog, leaped on top of Bob.

All at once, Bob and Molly gave loud screams. Mother ran into the hall to see what had happened.

Bob and Molly ran into the hall screaming that a monster was in the house. Into the hall Slob, the frog, hopped. Then came tiny Dot, the frog.

Bob and Molly realized their tricks had tricked each other.

Feed Words: just, under, bed.

LESSON 69

Phonics: Adding *ing*

When your student wanted to change layer-cake words by adding *ing, ed,* or *er,* he found that he had to drop the *e* frosting and add those new kinds of frostings.

Review spelling:

poke	poking	poked	poker
vote	voting	voted	voter
bake	baking	baked	baker
save	saving	saved	saver
wave	waving	waved	waver

Now that your student has met short-vowel words, he finds that something happens to these words when *ing, ed,* or *er* is added. These little words are so short they want to add an extra letter before the new endings get snapped on. The last letter is doubled before the suffix is placed on the word. Demonstrate: *hop, hopping, sit, sitting.*

You can dictate the following words: *jog, jogging, hop, hopping, fit, fitting, hit, hitting.*

Point out to your student that if that single-vowel word already has two consonants at the end, he does not have to add the extra letter. Example: *back, backing, toss, tossing, fill, filling.*

Warning: Many students have a terrible time with these suffixes. You may have to explain patiently this lesson several times. Review often.

LESSON 70

Phonics: Short u

One of the phonic integrals that can be introduced is *tion*. Due to lack of space in this book, this sound will be given very little attention.

In our language the sound of *sh* is repeated sometimes in the form of *ci, ti,* and *si* (*facial, partial, mansion*). Demonstrate the *tion* in *nation* and *station*.

The word *beautiful* is difficult for many students. I find it helps to suggest that the *a* is silent while *e* and *u* are long.

The short *u* sound can be associated with the first sound in *umbrella* or you can suggest that the short *u* has a disagreeable sound, *ugh*. Exaggerate the *u* to have a deep throat sound. Make a sour face and repeat the ugly sound of *ugh* just as dramatically as you did for the disagreeable sounds of *ack* and *ick*. Draw a big letter *u*, have a stick figure sweep something disagreeable down into the pit of the letter *u*. Now have your student repeat several times that low-down short *u* sound.

Give a spelling lesson from the list. Then reading can proceed. The two lessons after this are review for short *u*. Follow the usual lesson plan.

WORD LIST

cub	cud	cuff	bug	duck	dull
rub	mud	huff	dug	buck	gull
tub	suds	muff	hug	muck	hull
club		puff	jug	puck	lull
flub		bluff	lug	suck	
stub		stuff	mug	tuck	
shrub		gruff	rug	cluck	
		fluff	tug	pluck	
		scuff	plug	stuck	
		snuff	slug	struck	
			snug	truck	
			thug	chuck	
			chug		

pup	bus	but	crust	lunch
puppy	fuss	cut	dust	bunch
	Gus	hut	gust	
	Russ	mutt	must	
	plus	nut	rust	
		rut	trust	
		strut	just	

→

SILLY STORY

Tug Chug Was a Huge Truck

Big Chuck had a huge truck that he call<u>ed</u> Tug Chug. In the morning Big Chuck had to leave for work. He would lug his lunch pail to his truck. Then he would chuck his extra jacket in the front seat.

At last Big Chuck would stuff <u>him</u>self <u>be</u>hind the wheel of his huge truck. When it was cold <u>out</u>side Tug Chug, the truck, would just refuse to chug his motor. There was Big Chuck stuck in his truck. He would just have to call Gus and Russ, his friends, to help.

Soon Gus and Russ <u>ap</u>peared. After much fuss, Tug Chug would at last turn his motor over. The motor would puff and huff and at last <u>de</u>cide to run.

Russ and Gus would clap and cheer when Tug Chug and Big Chuck would finally drive down the street to work.

LESSON 71

Phonics: Short u (continued)

SILLY STORY

What Made Duck Cluck Sick?

My friend Duck Cluck would swim around in the sea as nice as could be. Not a thing would annoy Duck Cluck. Then one day a big storm came up. The wind blew so hard big waves tossed Duck Cluck up and down. The wind blew so hard and the waves tossed so much that Duck Cluck became sea sick.

Duck Cluck was feeling like he was about to be very sick. Then suddenly Duck Cluck's friend appeared. Duck Cluck's friend was Dudley, the sea gull. Dudley, the sea gull, flew around and around in the sky. He made loud gruff sounds. At last Dudley, the sea gull, shouted to Duck Cluck, "I am not surprised that you are sea sick. It is not the big waves that are making you sea sick. It is the junk in the water.

Duck Cluck cried back to Dudley, the sea gull, "Explain to me what you mean."

Dudley, the sea gull screamed, "From up here I can see a big mass of stuff floating in the water. There is a huge mass of scum. There is foam that seems to be soap suds. All this material is making you sick. Suddenly, Dudley, the sea gull became frightened. He shouted to his friend Duck Cluck, "Hurry, hurry, fly away as fast as you can."

Duck Cluck decided he would take Dudley's advice. Up, up, he flew just in time, for there on the dock was a huge truck unloading junk. Into the sea the truck dumped all kinds of dirty stuff.

Up in the air Duck Cluck began to feel fine. He realized that he was not sick any more.

Duck Cluck decided he would find a place in the sea that was clean. He would no longer stay near the dock. What a pity that the man in the truck did not care to keep the sea clean.

LESSON 72

Phonics: Short u (continued)

SILLY STORY

Mr. and Mrs. Thrush

The thrush is a beautiful bird that sings in the spring. You may have seen the thrush in the middle of spring. If you have shrubs and trees in your yard, you might see Mr. Thrush while he hops around in the grass. He just has a fine time plucking in the shrubs for bugs to eat.

Mr. Thrush has a rust color on the top of his head. The back of his head is rust color, too. His back and sides are light brown. On his tan tummy are dark brown spots. Mr. Thrush has a wife that is the same color, but her color is lighter all over.

Brown Thrush and his wife like to fly from tree to tree. However, they do not care to make their home in a tree. These birds make their snug homes in the shrubs.

Mr. and Mrs. Thrush tuck their little ones in their snug homes in the shrubs. These little ones seem to be just a ball of fluff. When these birds leave their homes to go out into the world, they are as large as mother and father. They are almost as large as Mr. and Mrs. Robin. However, they are more plump than the Robin family.

Mr. and Mrs. Thrush have a most beautiful song to sing. You must stop and listen this spring for the song of the thrush.

LESSON 73

Extra Words

There are several words that become exceptions to the silent *e* long-vowel, layer-cake words. Explain to your student that some of our English words can make us stumble. However, if we think carefully, we can manage them. *Some* and *come* and *none* have the same vowel sound. Then *gone* has *on* in it. Print these words on cards, keep reviewing them.

Your pupil has had the word *who* several times in the Feed Words. This word had the *wh* sound that is not quite like the *wh* in *when*. With enough repetition the differences in the sound fit into place.

Phonics: Short e

Some disabled readers need to take more time than is allotted in this book for each phonic integral. You have to be the judge of how fast the student can proceed. You may have to make up extra sentences using the Word Lists in each lesson.

Print the letters *m, n, l, f, x,* and *s*. These alphabet letters have sounds besides their alphabet names (example: *moan, note, load, fate, save*). They are the only consonants that can use their alphabet names in some words. Print the following words for your student to see: *stem, send, elk, Bess*. Notice the vowel in front of each of the letters. This is short *e*. Really, those alphabet letters should be *em, en, el, ex, ef, es*. Next time your student says the alphabet names of these letters, tell him to think about the short *e* that really should be in front.

In school, the teacher probably has a picture of an egg to remind the students of the short *e* sound in the word *egg*.

WORD LIST

den	gem	bell	less
hen	hem	fell	mess
Ken	stem	Nell	Bess
men	them	sell	dress
pen		tell	guess
ten	bet	well	nest
then	get	smell	best
when	jet	shell	pest
cent	let	jelly	rest
sent	met	held	west
bent	pet	weld	vest
dent	wet		guest
lent	Chet	egg	crest
went			
tent	kept		
plenty	slept		
lend	wept		
bend			
mend	left		
trend			

SILLY STORY

The Bell

Once upon a time a huge bell hung in a tiny church in a village called West Bend. Now this bell had not rung for years and years. One day when the bell ringer went to ring the bell for Ned and Nell's wedding, not a sound would come from the bell.

Somehow the gadget that the bell ringer had to bend to make the bell ring would not work. The gadget was bent, so the gadget would not let the bell ring.

Ned and Nell were wed but the church bell did not ring. Ned and Nell could never forget that when they were wed that church bell gadget was bent so the bell would not ring.

Ned and Nell worked hard after they were wed. They put money in the bank. Nell and Ned felt that everything in their life had gone so well that it was time to do something for their fellow men.

It came time for a friend* named Fred to be wed. Now was the time that Nell and Ned could do something for their fellow men.

Nell and Ned decided to take money out of the bank to mend the bend in the gadget that would ring the church bell.

So sure enough, before the day Fred was to be wed the beautiful bell in the church tower in West Bend was mended.

Ned and Nell had a fine celebration. They felt that when the church bell rang, the beautiful bell sound was for their wedding, too.

---

* NOTE: The letter *i* is silent in the word *friend*.

FIVE: DIGRAPHS AND EXTRA VOWEL INTEGRALS

LESSON 74

Phonics: Digraph *ph*

Your student has worked with the digraphs *ch*, *wh*, and *th*. Dyslexic students are apt to have auditory discrimination problems with *th* and the single letter *f*. To avoid confusion, I insist on a special exercise involving these sounds. Tell your student to repeat the *f* sound after you. Ask him where his tongue is sitting. (Answer: on the floor of his mouth.) Now he is to repeat the *th* sound. Where is his tongue? (Answer: just behind his upper teeth. If the tongue gets out in front of the teeth the student will have problems when pronouncing some *th* words.)

The dyslexic student may have trouble connecting a letter picture with these sounds. In each lesson for a while review these sounds and ask your pupil to print the letters involved. (Tall, skinny *f* can lie down on the floor of his mouth. Thick *th* presses in a thick feeling behind his front teeth.)

The next digraph to learn is *ph*. Once again we have two letters that have a sound that does not match *p* or *h*. The sound is just like *f*. Help your student decode the Word List. Can he print the words *phone*, *telephone*, *Philip*? (Give clues.) Have him underline the *ph* where he sees it.

WORD LIST

elephant   phone   telephone   telegraph   Philip

Phyllis   Ralph   autograph

SILLY STORY

An Elephant Friend

One day Ralph phoned the twins, Philip and Phyllis, to tell them that an elephant friend was coming to town.

Philip and Phyllis would not believe Ralph. They could not believe that Ralph had an elephant for a friend.

The twins asked Ralph where the elephant lived. Ralph said his elephant friend lived in Sarasota.

Philip was the nephew of a man who lived in Sarasota. Philip sent a telegraph to his uncle to ask about the elephant that was a friend of Ralph's.

Sure enough, there was an elephant who lived in Sarasota, who was going to visit Ralph.

Phyllis and Philip rushed over to Ralph's house to get his autograph. Surely Ralph would be famous when his elephant friend came to visit.

LESSON 75

Phonics: The *qu* pattern

The letter q is like the letter g but the monkey tail on q will curl up to try to reach the letter *u* that *always, always* insists on sitting beside *u*. Have your student practice the sound of *qu*. Then he is to print *qu* followed by these words: *quake, quite* (layer-cake words), *quail, queen* (peanut butter and jelly words). Point out to your pupil that the printed *q* in books just has a straight line its tail rests on. (The reason I teach the *q* with a right-hand curl is that this direction leads into the cursive writing the student will soon use.)

The Silly Story *Gail Quail* can be read in two installments. Several of the words have more than one syllable. Place a cover card over part of the word as your student decodes each section.

The word *instead* is used in this story. Your student has been introduced to the long *e* sound only of *ea*. In the next grade level of this program the sounds of *ea* are given detailed attention. (Example: *head, learn, bear, great.*)

Have your student underline the *qu* pattern.

WORD LIST

quake	quit
quite	quack
quail	quince
queen	quiet

SILLY STORY

Gail Quail

In Quebec a busy mother quail was scratching around the quince bushes. Mrs. Quail was trying to find her daughter, Gail. Ever since Gail Quail had been made Queen of the Quacking Club, her mother could never get her to work.

Before this time Gail Quail was the pride and joy of her family. Gail Quail was a quiet hard worker. She never quit work until she was quite sure she had done her share. Often Gail Quail would bring home such a large quantity of food, Mrs. Quail would not have to leave the nest for days.

Now all Gail Quail's fine habits had changed. In fact, now that Gail Quail was Queen of the Quacking Club of Quebec, she had begun to quarrel with her mother. Instead of being a quiet quail she had become a loud quacking quail.

Finally Gail Quail appeared under the quince bush. She asked her mother for a quiet conference. Mother Quail was puzzled. She just sat quietly.

Queen Gail Quail said in a loud quacking voice, "Mother, I no longer wish to live at home in the nest. In fact, I have decided I shall go out into the world and make my fortune."

That is exactly what Gail Quail did. She went out into the world and made a fortune. Gail Quail now lives happily in her own quiet nest in Quebec.

LESSON 76

Extra Words

The only sight words in this book the student cannot put into a phonic category at this point are: *put, said, would, could, should, to, too, do, does, done, come, some, gone, mother.*

You are going to add a new word that can be decoded. However, it gets misspelled so often that special consideration is due. The word is *their*. Explain that this new *their* tries to tell us something about the next word to it. Their home, their mittens, their pets, their toys. The other word *there* points out where something is, either *here* or *there*. This concept is hopelessly confusing for many students. If I had my way, I would not make the spelling correction until the seventh grade, when the student becomes neurologically mature enough to accept the abstraction. At that time I write these words in a column.

the
they
there
their

I underline *the* in each word and spend a few minutes each day in review. The words are rarely misspelled after that. However, the dyslexic in the second grade is not going to manage these words without a great deal of help.

Phonics: Long *o* sound for *ow*

We have a number of words in our language that end in the sound of long *o*. For some reason, most of the time we just will not let round *o* hang out at the end of a word. What we do is to let the letter *w* close in on *o*. Tell your student that when he sees the *ow* at the end of the word it is not going to use the sound he knows for *ow*. It will be long *o*, silent *w*. There are three words that are exceptions, but the nature of these three words lend themselves to be remembered. They are: *how, now, cow.*

Sentences for dictation: You should still be accentuating the special sounds of each phonic integral. When your pupil starts to misspell, repeat the sound, give him some hint. Try to get him to work the word out. (Example: ask if the vowel is short or long. If it is neither, ask what vowel pattern he thinks it is. Give him the associative ideas that have been described in the lesson.)

1. I will row my boat.
2. The crow can grow large.
3. Dave sat below the window.
4. That crow has flown away.
5. The snow will blow into the window.

The daily lesson following this one is a review. Follow the usual plan. Be sure to underline the phonics pattern in the words of the Silly Stories.

WORD LIST

bow	elbow	owe	own
low	shadow		sown
mow	window	growth*	blown
row	follow		grown
blow	borrow		flown
crow	sorrow		thrown*
flow	tomorrow		
glow	narrow		
grow			
slow			
snow			
show			
below			

* Notice that these last two columns of *ow*'s add an extra form to make life confusing!

→

SILLY STORY

Black Crow

Black Crow put something on his wings so he would glow in the dark. He wanted to show his friends how beautiful he was. Black Crow said he would borrow some magic paint so the other crows could paint the narrow part of their wings. Then these crow friends could follow him around and glow in the dark, also.

Black Crow liked to throw himself through the air. This crow would soar up into the air. Then he would dart down low. At times, Black Crow would slow down his flying so that he could get near Brown Cow, who stayed in the pasture.

Now Brown Cow did not like Black Crow. Brown Cow did not like to worry about whether Black Crow would swoop below her. Brown Cow did not want Black Crow to swoop between her legs.

Brown Cow would have been glad to throw snow balls at Black Crow. However, that was impossible because Brown Cow could not make snow balls.

One day Black Crow did a very low trick. He found some paint in a can that would glow in the dark. Very slowly he dipped his wings in the paint that glowed. Then Black Crow was prepared to show the world his new glowing wings.

That night Black Crow slowly soared up into the sky. When he flew himself down suddenly, his path looked like a flow of sparkling water through the sky.

Brown Cow was terrified. Brown Cow did not realize that the sparkling streak in the air was Black Crow. Brown Cow felt she wanted to throw herself into a hole to hide.

Black Crow did not realize that all this time Harlow, the farm boy, had been watching Black Crow slowly prepare the glow on his wings.

In the meantime Harlow, the farm boy, had been making a big pile of snow balls. When Black Crow began to show off the new glow on his wings, Harlow stood beside Brown Cow to protect her.

Harlow could throw the snow balls very high. Black Crow was very surprised to hear a snow ball whiz by him. Suddenly he became very scared when all those snow balls came whizzing past him.

Brown Cow was very grateful to Harlow, the farm boy. She gave him her best milk the very next day.

LESSON 77

Phonics: The new sound of *oo*

Have you been playing The Game? Your student has been using the *oo* sound of *boot*. Now you can explain that *oo* has a second sound, as in *look*. This word is in every beginning reading book, therefore your student may know it by sight. The teacher usually puts the word *look* on the board in large print. She then draws eyes, nose and mouth in the two *o*'s. The word *look* looks out at you. This sound is found in the following words: *foot, good, book, soot, hood, wool, look, took, cook, wood, stood, shook, brook, crook, hook.* Follow the usual lesson plan.

Sentences for dictation:

1. I like to read that good book.
2. Joan took a look at the cook.
3. I *would* like to have a pile of *wood*. (Homonyms.)
4. He shook the wool rug.
5. The crook stood on the curb.

SILLY STORY

Mrs. Wood

Mrs. Wood was a very good cook. Besides being a good cook, Mrs. Wood liked to sing. She stood in the middle of her kitchen and sang. She sang so loud the table shook.

This good jolly lady would cook and then she would sing. She would cook the brook trout and then she would hop from foot to foot while she sang.

One day a friend came to Mrs. Wood's house. This friend could hear the loud sound of the singing. This friend had eaten Mrs. Wood's good cooking but she had never been invited to hear Mrs. Wood's singing.

The friend stood on the door step and waited until the song was over. By this time Mrs. Wood's voice was so loud it began to shake the house. This friend decided she did not like the loud singing. She took one leap off the steps and dashed home to the peace and quiet of her home.

LESSON 78

Extra Words

The words *whether* and *weather* are misspelled by many students. When I ask new students to spell *whether*, they always ask, "Which one?" They confuse *whether* with *weather*. If you instruct your student to decode *whether* accurately, he will not confuse it with *weather* when in future phonics he meets the short e sound of *ea*.

Review the words *when* and *where*. Ask your student to repeat the *whe* sound after you. Then have him print that sound you give him. Ask him what short vowel he is dealing with. If he has a hard time associating the sound of *wh* (phoneme) with the printed letters (grapheme), be patient. He probably needs more review of *wh, th, ch, gh*, the consonant digraphs. The *th* sound of *whether* can be decoded and then the *er* (grapheme). (Notice I am adding new terminology for you!)

Phonics: The au, aw pattern

The *au, aw* sound is to be introduced. Tell your student that he has met the disagreeable sounds of some of the short vowels. Now he is going to learn about the sound of disappointment. Exaggerate the sound of *au*. When he says *au*, it sounds as if he were discouraged. The letter *a* has so many sounds by the time it latches onto *u* or *w* it really is discouraged. In fact, *a* would not mind tumbling right into the pit that the letter *u* makes. This is a good time to discuss what *daub* means (then have your pupil print it). Also discuss the difference between the words *haul* and *hall* (homonyms).

There are three Silly Stories in this lesson. You may need to take extra time for this material. Ask your student to underline the vowel patterns of *au* and *aw* if he is coordinated enough to do an accurate job.

Sentences for dictation:

1. Paul was hit by a daub of mud.
2. Paul will haul his boat to the water.
3. Saul will pause before he speaks.

1. What was the cause of his sickness?
2. Have you caught a fish?
3. The teacher taught Joe to sing.

1. The hawk makes an awful noise. (Review *oi, oy*.)
2. The hawk could crawl over the lawn.
3. Can the hawk yawn?

WORD LIST

law	daub	dawn	because
raw	haul	lawn	sauce
paw	maul	yawn	saucer
saw	Maud	brawl	fault
draw	Saul	crawl	vault
flaw	Paul	drawl	haunt
claw	fraud	shawl	gauze
straw	cause	awful	caught
bawl	pause	dawdle	taught
hawk	clause	awkward	haughty
			daughter

SILLY STORIES

A Daub of Mud That Hit Saul

Maud threw a daub of mud that hit Saul. Saul paused just a moment. Then he vaulted forward, to run after Maud. He caught up to naughty Maud and was about to bawl her out.

Saul said to Maud, "How could you be so awful to throw a daub of mud at me?"

In a haughty voice Maud said to Saul, "I saw you across the lawn. You gave a big yawn. You looked so awkward, I decided that a daub of mud would cause you to shut your mouth."

Saul said, "It was not my fault that I had to yawn. I think you played an awful trick. If I could, I would claw you into straw. You are the one who is awkward. In fact, your big fault is that you are a rude haughty naughty snob."

Paul and His Pet Hawk

Paul had a pet hawk. The hawk would hop around the lawn. Paul would haul a string over the lawn. When the pet hawk saw the string he would chase after Paul.

Over the lawn that hawk would crawl. At last Paul would pause to let the hawk catch the string. The hawk put out his claws and caught the string.

Paul smiled at his pet hawk when that hawk caught the string with his claws. Paul decided he would teach his black hawk a trick or two.

Paul threw a long straw in the air. Then he called to his pet hawk. He said, "Black hawk, use your claws to grab the straw."

Black hawk would just ignore Paul. He would just hop over the lawn.

Paul's friend Saul came over the lawn. He asked Paul if he had taught the black hawk a trick. Paul gave a yawn. He said, "This black hawk does not understand me yet. I have taught my dog tricks but it will take time to teach this black hawk."

After a big yawn Paul said to Saul, "I am tired of teaching my hawk. Let's play ball."

Naughty Maud

A drowsy clown heard a shout. He woke up to find the cause. It was Maud, the haughty daughter of Mr. Saul.

The drowsy clown gave a yawn and began to crawl off his couch.

Maud was making a wicked racket. She shouted, she growled and howled. Then she hooted and blew a horn.

The clown was no longer drowsy, he was annoyed. Why should that naughty haughty Maud create such a racket? The clown was bound he ought to bawl Maud out for making such a racket.

Clown screamed to Maud, "If you growl or howl or drawl or bawl one more moment, I shall take a huge piece of gauze and haul it around your mouth."

Sour haughty naughty Maud paused just long enough to pout. Then she scooted off the lawn and bounded down the street.

CONCLUSION

Your student has now completed the major phonic integrals. There are several other units he needs to learn. However, he now has a decoding ritual that he can use in any future work. New phonics work should cover problems like *ive* (*give, massive*), *ude* (*crude*), *mn* (*autumn*), *ea* (*head, bear, learn*), *ou* (*couple*), *ei, ie* (*eight, receive, believe*), silent letters *wr, gn, kn, h, gh, gu* (as in *write, honest, ghost, guess*), along with the rest of the *ough* words, plurals and contractions, and a few other sticklers. Also, the entire concept of syllabication should be carefully explained.

By the time you have completed this book, your student either has automated his reading or automated much of it. Rereading the stories and getting books from the library for practice reading will nudge your student into the magic of automation. Remember that practice on a daily basis is the only solution to mastery of any skill.

Those of you who have disciplined yourselves to complete this book deserve special praise. Your reward, of course, is to see that magic I, too, have experienced when the student progresses from a nonreader to a reader and speller who can compete with his peers in the classroom.

APPENDIX

How Does the Integral Phonics Reading Program Differ Technically
from Other Programs?

The procedures used in the Integral Phonics Reading Program have been designed to complement the neurological development of the student whose nervous system may not work at optimal efficiency. Although I am not a neurologist, I am a teacher who feels strongly that educators need to use the research neurologists have made available. We who want desperately to help the people who have difficulty in learning to read and to spell search in many areas for tools that will assure reading success. It seems logical that those who have studied brain function can give clues that are needed by educators.

R. M. N. Crosby, M.D., tells us that "reading is the most complex and difficult neurological assignment a person is called upon to perform in his lifetime, exceeding in difficulty even the involved task of learning to speak."[1]

Adults realize that the child learns to speak a language after daily exposure to the communicating people around him. He acquires his skill without using any conscious effort. Constant bombardment of language eventually stimulates the child to process speech sounds. At the time when the child learns to read, he must develop a type of processing he has never exerted before. Now we demand from him the conscious effort of analyzing and synthesizing individual sounds.[2] He must have perfectly synchronized brain circuits to meet success in reading and writing. For those who may have less than efficient brain pathways, the mastery of language arts becomes a discouraging struggle.

I worked with disabled readers many years before I stumbled upon the sensitive work that Samuel Torrey Orton did in the field of reading disorders. I had realized there were a consid-

---

[1] R. M. N. Crosby, M.D., with Robert A. Liston, *The Waysiders* (New York: Delacort Press, 1968), p. 13.
[2] Aleksandr Romanovich Luria, *Higher Cortical Functions in Man* (New York: Basic Books, 1968), p. 408.

erable number of individuals who had good intellectual ability but were crippled readers. Orton's book, *Reading, Writing, and Speech Problems in Children,* made me understand that I could find medical information that would corroborate all the empirical evidence I had experienced. The book by the English neurologist MacDonald Critchley, *The Dyslexic Child,* told me that these disabled readers were being designated as dyslexic. Some educators have fought this term. For me to label or not to label is unimportant. We must get on with the business of finding ways to help the disabled readers. Educators are completely frustrated when they face the statistics that reveal the numbers of functional illiterates in our affluent society.

I have observed that when the so-called dyslexic student tries to process words, analysis and synthesis of phonetic integrals become a confusing maze. For the word *mail* he may say *mile.* If you point your pencil to the long *a* and ask him to repeat the letter, he will give you the correct sound of the *a.* Then when he goes to blend the *m* with the *a,* any vowel sound may come out. He might say *meal, mile,* or *mal.*

Teachers who have seen students struggle with phonetic blending conclude there must be an easier way for the child to cope with the printed words. They may in confusion turn to the look-and-say method, thinking that by giving intensive exposure to the list of words most often used in basal readers the disabled reader will eventually acquire reading skill.

I have found that unless the dyslexic student learns to master the synthesizing process, which has to be done by a phonetic-phonic method, he does not learn to read well and his spelling is hopeless. The method of teaching these students in the Integral Phonics Reading Program differs from other methods in one specific area. When the student starts, he is instructed to focus on the first vowel in the one-syllable, long-vowel word. He must pronounce this vowel out loud before he takes the next step, that of voicing the first consonant and blending it to the first long vowel. This vocalizing process is not a device extrapolated from a hypothetical premise; the entire procedure evolved on a trial-and-error basis to an eventual solution to the difficulty met by dyslexic students when they attempted vowel processing.

A. R. Luria's research gives explanations that coincide with the empirical evidence I have accumulated. At one point he states that in the initial stages of education the child has great difficulty with phonetic analysis if he is prohibited from articulating the components of a word.[3]

In the IPRP, the Seven Special Steps describe the articulating action that is used with every word during the time the disabled reader is learning the decoding skill. These steps must be performed by a conscious effort. The procedure seems to help overcome the erratic guessing, as described by Luria,[4] that overwhelms many students while they process the individual words. Throughout the whole Integral Phonics Reading Program, procedures have been refined so that a minimal work load is placed on the auditory and visual analyzing and synthesizing systems.

My experience in teaching non-English-speaking students to read English has reinforced my premise of the need to repeat the correct vowel sound aloud before the student tries to blend the consonant to it. The student is confused when he starts learning the English sounds of vowels. The Spanish letter *a* sounds like the English pattern *ar.* The student is helped to pronounce the English long *a.* He repeats this long *a* several times. Then he is asked to look at

---

[3] Ibid., p. 409.

[4] Ibid., p. 378.

the word *bake* and repeat it out loud. Invariably the word comes out *bark*. You then point to the long *a* and ask him what the sound is in English. The student will repeat it correctly only to revert back to the *ar* sound when he tries the whole word, *bake*. He, just like his English-speaking classmate who is learning to read, has to have exercises in the blending of the *ba* before he can proceed to form the whole word correctly.

Observing these students who are not dyslexic learn to read a new language, along with becoming familiar with Luria's research, has made me feel that a large number of our population must process on a *conscious* level the words they learn to read even though some may complete this task so rapidly that the teacher is unaware the conscious activity takes place.

Having the student focus on and then vocalize the first vowel rather than the first letter of a word will be questioned by those who have worked with the disabled reader. Knowing the dyslexic student has a left-right directional problem, you may think the Seven Special Steps add to rather than correct confusion. I shall welcome your observations after you try the process. The neurologist may be able to explain why the procedure works.

How Can the IPRP Help Various Types of Reading Disability?

I have become particularly interested in the fact that the use of the Seven Special Steps seems to be the key to the correction of a variety of reading, writing, and spelling disabilities. There are students who have difficulty distinguishing between similar-sounding letters such as *b* and *p, d* and *t,* etc. There are others who perceive similar letters inaccurately, such as *x* for *k,* or *m* for *n.* Still other students have difficulty blending letters together. These are only three of the types of difficulties that may be evident individually or collectively in the disabled reader.

I have found that regardless of the type of reading and spelling disorder, the student overcomes his problem by using the Seven Special Steps along with the procedure of indirect memorization of sounds and symbols as described in the daily lessons.

Whether these steps have some relationship to each processing system in the brain involved in reading and spelling, or whether they act as an integrating mechanism, I leave to the neurologist to ponder.